FLORENCE S.C.
77
11

19
22
Coca-Cola

Quarto.com

First Published in 2024 by Motorbooks, an imprint of The Quarto Group,
100 Cummings Center, Suite 265-D, Beverly, MA 01915, USA.
T (978) 282-9590 F (978) 283-2742

Motorbooks titles are also available at discount for retail, wholesale, promotional, and bulk purchase. For details, contact the Special Sales Manager by email at specialsales@quarto.com or by mail at The Quarto Group, Attn: Special Sales Manager, 100 Cummings Center, Suite 265-D, Beverly, MA 01915, USA.

28 27 26 25 24 1 2 3 4 5

ISBN: 978-0-7603-8878-5

Digital edition published in 2024
eISBN: 978-0-7603-8879-2

Library of Congress Cataloging-in-Publication Data

Names: Branham, H. A., author. | Cain, Holly, author.
Title: NASCAR mavericks : the rebels and racers who revolutionized stock car racing / H.A. Branham, Holly Cain ; foreword by Tony Stewart ; afterword by Ross Chastain.
Description: Beverly, MA : Motorbooks, 2024. | Includes index. | Summary: "NASCAR Mavericks recounts the legendary drivers, team owners, wrenches, races, and events that have made NASCAR America's favorite motorsport for more than 75 years"— Provided by publisher.
Identifiers: LCCN 2024018638 | ISBN 9780760388785 | ISBN 9780760388792 (ebook)
Subjects: LCSH: Stock car drivers—United States—Biography. | Stock car racing—United States—History. | NASCAR (Association)—History.
Classification: LCC GV1032.A1 B73 2024 | DDC 796.72092/273—dc23/eng/20240514
LC record available at https://lccn.loc.gov/2024018638

Design: Cindy Samargia Laun
Cover Image: NASCAR; Front endpaper: RacingOne/Getty Images; Back endpaper: NASCAR

Printed in China

NASCAR® MAVERICKS

The Rebels and Racers Who Revolutionized Stock Car Racing

H. A. Branham /// Holly Cain
Foreword by Tony Stewart /// Afterword by Ross Chastain

motorbooks

CONTENTS

ACKNOWLEDGMENTS

In any undertaking such as this, you better have help. I got plenty from co-author Holly Cain. And we both benefited from big-time assistance from people throughout the industry. Start with the Foreword-Afterword team we came up with. Tony Stewart and Ross Chastain. We asked. They agreed. Many thanks to those two mavericks.

Their help was indicative of what we encountered. The overall response was overwhelming—and greatly appreciated. And, in some cases, it also was pretty humbling. Take this case: Sterling Marlin, slowed by Parkinson's, doing a phone interview to talk about the infamous L. W. Wright's 1982 scam job. Or this one: an eighty-five-year-old Bill Brodrick, the legendary UNOCAL "Hat Man" who ran Victory Lane ceremonies for years, firing off classic insights from the classic years of the NASCAR Cup Series. One more: ninety-four-year-old Tiger Tom Pistone, on the phone, recounting for the zillionth time the story of him having an oxygen tank and mask in his car at the 1960 Daytona 500 because he was afraid of wrecking and landing in Lake Lloyd, in the Daytona International Speedway infield.

Thanks to those three, and to the many others who helped build our stories: drivers, owners, crew chiefs, NASCAR executives, and media members. Also, NASCAR historian Buz McKim gets credit for laying the story foundations. He wrote the introductions for each chapter.

A nod as well to Motorsports Hall of Fame of America President George Levy for developing the original concept of *NASCAR Mavericks*. And a thanks to the NASCAR Archives and Research Center and NASCAR Research Assistant Kate Sayers, for photography that brought the concept to life.

Let's attempt to touch a few more bases:

Thanks to Mary Cassells for her initial round of editing . . . to Motorbooks' Zack Miller, our day-to-day contact during the project . . . to Brooke Pelletier, our Motorbooks project manager . . . to NASCAR Chairman and CEO Jim France, who gave a hearty thumbs-up to this deal—and then gave us two interviews.

Cheers, to all,

H. A. Branham
April 2024

DEDICATION

For William Noah King, who left this world in 2024 at the age of 16, but lives on in the hearts of so many throughout the NASCAR community.

FOREWORD

TONY STEWART

What does it mean to be a maverick? Speaking from personal experience, it's doing what you think is right, even when others say you're wrong. And it's being told you can't, so you go even harder just to prove them wrong.

Racing is filled with mavericks. Whether it's on some short track in the middle of nowhere, or on the biggest and brightest stage, everybody wants to beat everybody. The drivers buckle in to beat every other driver in the race, and the mechanics who put the race cars together do it intent on outworking and outsmarting the competition.

Whether you're holding a steering wheel or a wrench, you need to have an independent streak to find success. Now, it needs to be balanced with getting along with people, because you need a team to achieve consistent results. But doing what everyone else is doing doesn't win championships. It might get you a victory here or there, but sustained success is not built on the status quo.

You need that maverick mentality—a way that breaks the mold. The way Steve Kinser won twenty World of Outlaws Sprint Car Series championships. The way Alan Kulwicki proved a driver/owner could win a NASCAR Cup Series title. The way Roger Penske obliterated the Indy 500 field in 1994 with an engine that made two hundred more horsepower than anyone else. The way Ray Evernham reinvented how stock cars could be built and how pit crews could be trained. The way Richard Petty, Dale Earnhardt, and Jimmie Johnson each won seven NASCAR Cup Series championships.

There are more mavericks, for sure. Some are out front, some are behind the scenes. Some, like me, who after forty-three years of racing in circles, decided racing in a straight line at 330 mph with an 11,000-horsepower engine behind their head was an appropriate career change.

It's about being unconventional, and getting comfortable being uncomfortable. Being a maverick isn't easy but it's damn satisfying.

Tony Stewart never minced words with his fellow NASCAR drivers. You sort of always knew where he stood.

INTRODUCTION

WHEN THE TITLE of this book was first proposed, my first, immediate, reaction was that *NASCAR Mavericks* seemed perfect—and redundant. After all, NASCAR, at its core, is all about the maverick concept, whatever that is at *its* core. Hell, one could argue they're almost synonyms.

The dictionary defines a maverick as an unorthodox or independent-minded person.

Yeah, that'll work.

Mavericks are deeply woven into NASCAR's fabric. They are the oldest threads, yet the strongest and certainly the most interesting. From the outset, NASCAR's innate appeal was founded on the everyman who did things on their own, their way. A natural progression from the sport's 1930s and '40s roots on Southeastern baked red dirt tracks and backroad moonshine-running paths.

And so, of course, there would be no shortage of material for these pages. Neither would there be a shortage of opinions on who or what qualifies as a NASCAR Maverick. Interviews inevitably turned into mini lectures at times. It was like signing up for Stock Car History 101, repeatedly. None other than NASCAR Chairman Jim France even offered some prime suggestions.

Good news: There was plenty of agreement among plenty of folks about our choices. On the other hand, some of our mavericks might seem a bit surprising. Admittedly, there were curveballs. Again, there was a lot to choose from.

(ABOVE) **David Pearson has the outside line on a restart for the 1976 Daytona 500. Pearson went on to win the race for the only time in his career.**

(OPPOSITE) **Talladega Superspeedway opened in 1969, becoming the largest oval track to host NASCAR races, at 2.66 miles with turns banked at thirty-three degrees—Daytona on steroids. Drivers checked it out and then boycotted due to safety concerns. Bill France Sr. ran the race anyway, with a field of non-descript competitors.**

When looking for a co-author, there was only one choice—the indomitable Holly Cain, for years, one of the nation's very best motorsports journalists. Once upon a time she was a bit of a maverick herself, as was I. There will be no further word on that but suffice it to say that NASCAR has been a good longtime fit for us both.

NASCAR Mavericks spotlights the trailblazers, risk takers, forward thinkers, and out-and-out hell-raisers responsible for breakthroughs and advances that formed, shaped, and, eventually, defined NASCAR. We also look beyond the people behind the wheel or under the hood, to the actual machines and the actual places, in some cases, where they raced. Cars have, indeed, been stars in NASCAR. So have monumental events that were held in true maverick style—a bit dodgy around the edges but all with the greater down-the-road good in mind. Or something like that.

This book is not designed to rehash history. Stories on the most recognizable subjects especially strive to "rework the angle" as the old newspaper term goes. Often, actual racin' takes a backseat to personal asides, funny stories, behind-the-scenes happenings. Make of that what you will, but it seemed like the only way to go, because mavericks require a personal context to make their stories sing.

For so many fans, their initial attraction to NASCAR was its down-home charm, its inherent quirkiness, its celebration of motor-driven eccentricity, that it seemed like every race was a convention of characters hell-bent on going fast and getting somewhere in life in the process.

NASCAR Mavericks, then, should serve as a reminder of that attraction.

Yeah, that'll work.

14
Parks
14

THE 1940s

PRECEDENTS FOR BOLDNESS TO COME

NASCAR's official timeline has it being founded December 14 through 17, 1947, with its first race held on February 15, 1948.

CORRECT ON BOTH ACCOUNTS but considerably misleading; the National Association for Stock Car Auto Racing, as an entity, indeed, has those dates as historical markers. As a concept, swimming around in the brain of "Big Bill" France, NASCAR actually was dated by then.

Various stock car organizations—or attempts at such—existed before and after NASCAR came into being. And all of those attempts featured promoters, car owners, mechanics, crew chiefs, and, of course, race car drivers who were unknowingly plotting a course for the future of the sport by providing France all the examples required—both good and bad—to plot his own sanctioning strategy.

Mavericks were everywhere, many of them past or present moonshiners, some with outsized legends built not solely on facts. Drivers like Lloyd Seay, who France called the best racer he'd ever seen, who people swore they saw drive a hot rod straight up a pine tree.

The abundance of mavericks was good news and bad news.

NASCAR hit the ground fueled by the maverick spirit—or spirits—when France finally wrested control of a sport that was fractured, unorganized, and at times corrupt with payouts and rules, in some cases, nowhere to be found.

There was a lot to get your arms around.

France's vision was of a true national championship-level series with showroom cars, slightly modified, attracting everyday Americans who could identify with such machines. That was the ticket. Always had been, in his mind. This was "win on Sunday, sell on Monday" in its infancy.

At the outset of the December 1947 meetings, France laid it out to the attendees. This never gets old:

> *Stock car racing has got distinct possibilities for Sunday shows and we do not know how big it can be if it's handled properly. . . . I believe stock car racing can become a nationally recognized sport by having a National Point Standing. Stock car racing as we've been running it is not, in my opinion, the answer. . . . We must try to get track owners and promoters interested in building stock car racing up. We are all interested in one thing, that is, improving the present conditions. The answer lies in our group right here today to do it.*

NASCAR would have two years remaining in the 1940s to start doing it. It was a whirlwind.

(PREVIOUS) **Parks and his driver, Bob Flock, confer before the start of a Modified race at Greenville-Pickens Speedway (Easley, South Carolina) in 1946.**

(OPPOSITE) **The year is 1949, the race is the NASCAR Cup Series debut at now-iconic North Wilkesboro Speedway. It's the season finale for the new series, then called Strictly Stock. The '49 series champion Red Byron is in the mix, driving the No. 22.**

20
14
MOYER SPECIAL
BALTO. MARYLAND
LINCOLN-MERCURY
DEALER
22

Bill France Sr., in all his 1950s glory, majestically surveying his kingdom of sand, surf, and speed.

BILL FRANCE SR.

REGARDING "MAVERICKS" and NASCAR, there can be no other place to start, no other person to start with, than William Henry Getty France—Bill France Sr., "Big Bill," all 6 foot 5 inches (1 m 93 cm) of over-the-top enthusiasm that bordered on bluster but was always rooted in reality, even if it didn't seem so at the time.

"Big Bill" is the *OM*: Original Maverick.

From *OM*, all mavericks have flowed and will continue to flow as long as there's a red-white-and-blue heartbeat left in what one of the greatest American journalists, Tom Brokaw, called "the greatest American sport."

The man was a maverick from the outset, especially when it came to relocating in Florida. Some folks thought he had, perhaps, lost it, moving from his hometown, Washington, DC, in 1934 to some hill jack place called Daytona Beach—in the middle of the Great Depression no less—with less than $100 in his pocket.

He drove a car called a Hupmobile, pulling a self-built trailer containing a modest collection of belongings. The attraction was two-fold: good weather and racing. For France, it was personal *and* pragmatic. He was a mechanic and had grown weary of winter and icy garage floors beneath cars. He was also a racer, of sorts, his main indoctrination coming on treacherous board tracks in the Northeast, like the one in Laurel, Maryland.

Laurel Speedway was a 1.18-mile wooden oval. If a car crashed and burned, so might a portion of the track. The racing was rough, real, and just what a young man needed to spark his racing desire. When "Big Bill" was in his teens, the owners of Laurel let him drive the family Model T around the oval. He was hooked.

Daytona Beach had it all. Back then, the beach was famous for annual land speed record runs—the precursors to NASCAR's annual Speed Weeks at Daytona International Speedway. Sir Malcolm Campbell, Daytona's first racing superstar, driving the otherworldly (at the time) Bluebirds, chasing a 300-mph run on the famous hard-packed shoreline sands in Daytona.

(LEFT) **"Big Bill" and Annie B.—Bill France Sr. and Anne Bledsoe France—pose on the sands of Daytona in the 1930s, with no idea of the wonders to come in the world of big-time auto racing.**

(BELOW) **Bill France Sr. got his early racing start at tracks in Maryland, in cars like the Ford Model T, shown here in 1931. Soon, he would gravitate to stock cars and become one of the country's best racers.**

Yes, good weather and racing, that's what drove France to drive his wife Anne and young son Bill Jr.—NASCAR's future leader—to Florida. Forget the old tale about the Hupmobile crapping out, stranding the family. France was a mechanic. He would've fixed the car if needed.

"Annie, this is it!" France shouted when the Hupmobile puttered onto State Road A1A, Florida's coastal road.

Was it ever.

(ABOVE LEFT) **In the mid-1930s, Bill France Sr. opened an AMOCO service station on Main Street in Daytona Beach. It became a hub for racing types. It remains open as "316 Main Street Station" and is a popular destination for race fans visiting Daytona Beach.**

(ABOVE RIGHT) **A dapper Bill France Sr. in the 1940s, when NASCAR was still a gleam in his eye and a dream in his mind.**

"BIG BILL" FRANCE had the size and enthusiasm to get people's attention, but his self-assuredness is what kept it.

"When it came to Bill France Sr., everything was always going to work," his daughter-in-law, Betty Jane France, recalled. "That's the way it was with him."

Betty Faulk, his longtime executive assistant—secretary, in those days—said "Big Bill" didn't need to work a room upon arrival. He filled it, all by himself.

"Senior could talk people into everything, had people giving him money to build everything," Faulk said. "Senior would walk into a room and people would just do what he wanted. I once saw the Kennedys up close, and they had that same kind of charisma. It just emanated from them. Senior was that way."

Other employees were similarly awed, especially at their first sighting. "Like meeting a mountain," said one.

He kept racing for a while, becoming one of the country's very best stock car drivers before quitting in 1946 to concentrate on promoting races. "Big Bill" the racer became "Big Bill" the salesman.

In 1947, he operated another stock car series, the National Championship Stock Car Circuit (NCSCC), which proved to be the setup pitch for the high, hard one: NASCAR.

From December 14 through 17, 1947, he more or less manhandled the sport of stock car racing, bringing a large group of the sport's leaders to Daytona Beach for a series of meetings during which NASCAR was founded. He was approved as the organization's first president, almost as an afterthought according to the meeting minutes.

He came out of retirement for only one NASCAR race: July 4, 1948, at Martinsville (Virginia) Speedway, just down the road from his DC birthplace, in a berg called Horse.

And that was that, one eighth-place finish. France had a sport to build.

He introduced the concept of true stock car racing in 1949, showroom sedans to slightly modified race cars, sparking the "win on Sunday, sell on Monday" concept that added to NASCAR's All-American appeal.

In NASCAR's very first Strictly Stock Division event, June 19, 1949, in Charlotte, North Carolina, he disqualified the original winner then had a lawsuit challenging his decision dismissed. There would be no messing with his rule book or, sometimes, with "Big Bill" himself when it came to competition decisions. Sometimes in those days, he took to carrying a pistol or wearing one on his belt, just to reinforce the point.

He begged and borrowed—and sold, again—two decades later, to complete the construction of his dream racetrack, the 2.5-mile Daytona International Speedway in 1959, to finally get racing off the beach, out of the past, and aimed at the future.

Not satisfied, he built a bigger, faster track in Alabama—Talladega Superspeedway—ten years after that. That same year, he co-founded the International Motor Sports Association (IMSA), bringing structure to sports car racing.

In 1971, he and his son Bill Jr., acting on a Junior Johnson deal brokerage, started NASCAR's landmark sponsorship with R. J. Reynolds Tobacco that would create the NASCAR Winston Cup Series that lasted until 2003.

And in 1972, he stepped down making Bill France Jr. NASCAR's second president. Bill Sr. continued to lead NASCAR's sister company, the International Speedway Corporation.

"Bill Jr. was given the reins to fashion the sport," said NASCAR's third president, Mike Helton.

France was en route to becoming, arguably, the nation's top stock car driver when he won a 160-mile race on the Daytona Beach and Road Course in July 1940.

(RIGHT) **One of the most iconic NASCAR pictures showing Bill France Sr. heading a table of stock car notables from throughout the country during the December 14 through 17, 1947, meetings that resulted in the founding of NASCAR. The meetings took place at the Streamline Hotel's second-floor Ebony Lounge. The Streamline was restored in the 2010s and reimagined as a boutique hotel—with a NASCAR theme.**

(OPPOSITE) **The definitive photo, shot in 1955, of the legendary Daytona Beach and Road Course's last incarnation, 4.2 miles. Four years later the course would be history, replaced by Daytona International Speedway several miles east.**

HILLSIDE CEMETERY in Ormond Beach, Florida, is tucked into a middle-class neighborhood, just a short walk from the Atlantic shoreline. Just inside a softly shaded entrance lies Bill France Sr. and his wife Annie B. She went first, on January 2, 1992, due to a stroke. Bill Sr. followed on July 7, finally succumbing to the ravages of Alzheimer's disease.

The gravesite is best visited in the evening . . . a light rain, even better . . . when the cemetery is less likely to have others on the property. The visit must be quiet, as sedate as possible. There is much to reflect upon, starting with the sheer dichotomy of seeing this great man at rest after his lifetime of nonstop action.

In the 1960s, during one of his legendary Bahamian fishing trips, he and longtime NASCAR/ISC (International Speedway Corporation) executive Jim Foster were relaxing—and reflecting.

"You know, Jim, it hasn't been all bad, has it?" France asked Foster. "No, Bill. It's been great, and it's going to be a lot better," replied Foster.

Call Foster a prophet—with a sense of humor, perhaps. When one walks through the Hillside Cemetery gate nearest the France graves, they are greeted by a large headstone, the first one you see, on the immediate right. It is Jim Foster's grave.

Foster is on the pole, forever.

It's comforting to think about "Big Bill" France being somewhere, laughing about that one.

(continues on page 24)

THE DEBUT

AS 1948 DAWNED, NASCAR founder "Big Bill" France seemed bigger than ever, with momentum in tow. NASCAR had been formed in December 1947; now France needed a dynamic first season to get his new organization underway, although with tempered expectations.

A bit of a dilemma loomed. France's brainchild of "Strictly Stock" racing for NASCAR's inaugural season wasn't going to work, just yet. During World War II, consumer automobiles were, of course, not a priority, and in 1948 manufacturers were faced with making up for that production lull. There just weren't enough sedans to go from showroom to racetrack.

On the upside, there were many modifieds ready to go racin', mainly 1939 Ford Coupes. Powered by the Ford flathead V8, in addition to being plentiful, the cars were cheap to fix and easy to enhance for performance. That's why moonshine runners in the Southeast loved them.

FIRST NASCAR SANCTIONED RACE IN 1948

8TH ANNUAL

DAYTONA BEACH

MODIFIED

STOCK CAR CLASSIC

Sunday, February 15, 1948

150-Mile Race on the New 2.2-Mile Stock Car Championship Road-Beach Course

National Association Stock Car Auto Racing Inc.

NASCAR

NATIONAL HEADQUARTERS, 29 GOODALL AVE., DAYTONA BEACH, FLORIDA

PRESIDENT—BILL FRANCE COMMISSIONER—E. G. "CANNONBALL" BAKER

— Affiliates —

AMERICAN STOCK CAR RACING ASSOCIATION, INC. — TRENTON, N. J.

OHIO SPEEDWAY ASSOCIATION, INC. — BEREA, OHIO

CHATTANOOGA RACING ASSOCIATION — CHATTANOOGA, TENN.

— Racing Classification —

STRICTLY STOCK • MODIFIED STOCK • ROADSTERS

"AUTO RACING THAT IS OPEN TO EVERYONE"

Why not join an association that gives every one an opportunity to take part in the country's growing sport of stock car racing? We welcome all those who want to become part of a national organization. Competition memberships and associate memberships open to all persons who drive an automobile. You may be eligible for NASCAR sanctioned events which include: Speed Trials on Daytona Beach—Racing on the new Road-Beach Course—Sanctioned races on all types of tracks—National Roadster Championship on Daytona Beach.

FOR FULL INFORMATION WRITE TODAY TO NATIONAL HEADQUARTERS

(RIGHT) **The main promotional flier for the first NASCAR race, February 15, 1948, on a 2.2-mile beach and road course.**

(OPPOSITE) **Lee Morgan, in the No. 8 Ford modified, leads a pack through the treacherous South Turn on the Daytona Beach and Road Course, in NASCAR's 1948 debut. Morgan finished seventh.**

France recalibrated and assembled a fifty-two-race schedule for those mods. The debut was set for February 15, 1948, in Daytona Beach on a new 2.2-mile beach-road course, now farther south along the Atlantic shoreline, running 1 mile south on the imperfect two-lane A1A pavement and a much wilder mile back north, plowing through the sand and, sometimes, avoiding the surf. This layout was about 1 mile shorter than the previous one, sure to increase close quarters and fender-rubbing competition.

NASCAR was an unknown, facing this certainty: Dreams, ideas, and sheer moxie were going to be tested.

This had better work, many had to be saying. The Daytona Beach and Road Course was no longer a one-off.

"I have to think that the first NASCAR race was vital," said Buz McKim, former historian at the NASCAR Hall of Fame. "It had to succeed . . . but I think that, generally, it was a given that it would."

The main reason for optimism? France himself.

"Remember, he knew how to promote," McKim said. "Big Bill also had his stars from the old National Championship Stock Car Circuit ready to go, and he certainly had momentum on his side. It also helped that they had been racing on the beach for quite a while."

Sixty-two drivers entered this first event, advertised on a promotional poster as the "8th Annual Daytona Beach Modified Stock Car Classic," the title inclusive of the pre-NASCAR February races held on the previous beach-road course. The word "modified" is printed in conspicuously smaller type than the rest of the title copy. It looks strange, as if done in error. Chances are it was no mistake. Just a hunch.

The race carried an additional title: The Rayson Memorial. In pre-NASCAR days, France named the beach-road event in honor of British Royal Air Force pilot Edward Knowles Rayson, a former Grand Prix racer killed in a 1939 airplane crash in England.

Approximately fourteen thousand fans watched NASCAR history unfold, fifty cars starting the sixty-eight-lap race, for the bargain ticket price of $2.50. Legendary local sportswriter Benny Kahn of the *Daytona Beach News-Journal* described the crowd as "a small army . . . as thick as seeds on a loaf of rye bread."

Some seeds saw no sense in shelling out even that modest ticket fee, finding routes through the thick Palmetto scrub to trackside vantage points. The stories are true: France had signs warning of rattlesnakes lurking in said scrub erected at various spots along the course to scare off those nonpaying scalawags. The actual existence of trackside rattlesnakes was never confirmed.

Can't make it up.

Same goes for the storybook ending to NASCAR's first big race day, with World War II hero Red Byron, of Talladega, Alabama, driving a '39 Ford for Raymond Parks, winning. Byron got $1,000—total purse was $3,500—and 175 points toward the inaugural NASCAR National Championship that he also ended up capturing after eleven victories in the fifty-two-race season.

Byron was racing in those days despite a serious leg injury suffered during the war when his Army Air Corps bomber was shot down. Master crew chief/mechanic Red Vogt made it possible, designing an innovative extended clutch pedal bolted to Byron's leg brace, enabling him to change gears despite the injury.

Vogt, already known as a wrench man extraordinaire for his tree-shade accomplishments in the moonshine business, was en route to becoming, perhaps, stock car racing's first garage superstar. Made sense. Either or, the guy made cars go fast.

And he was starting 1948 on some kind of roll. Two months earlier, as part of the contingent that gathered in Daytona Beach to form a new stock car organization, Vogt was the one who suggested NASCAR for the organization's name.

Byron bested a field of fifty to win the race that showcased then-current and future stars: 1947 National Championship Stock Car Circuit champion Fonty Flock, Curtis Turner, Jim Paschal, Buck Baker, and Daytona Beach native Marshall Teague, who finished second behind Byron. Top finishers avoided the inevitable frenzy: five South Turn wrecks, one on the North Turn, and a triple barrel roll on the pavement stretch of the course—but no serious injuries.

Kahn called ol' Red "Lord Byron," writing that he was a "wounded war veteran with a racing heart as big as a steering wheel."

An unfortunate footnote in terms of NASCAR history is the apparent and inadvertent dismissal of 1948's opener—and the '48 season overall. The 1949 season featured the awaited debut of the Strictly Stock Division with the first Strictly Stock race on June 19, 1949 at Charlotte Speedway. In the minds of many fans, *that* has become the generally recognized first-ever NASCAR race. One can even find it referenced as "the start of NASCAR" despite it taking place sixteen months later than the real thing.

Unfortunate, indeed. France had the cars, the stars—and the future—all wrapped up into one outlandish, surf-and-sun splashed package on February 15, 1948. Something that should never be forgotten, much less overshadowed.

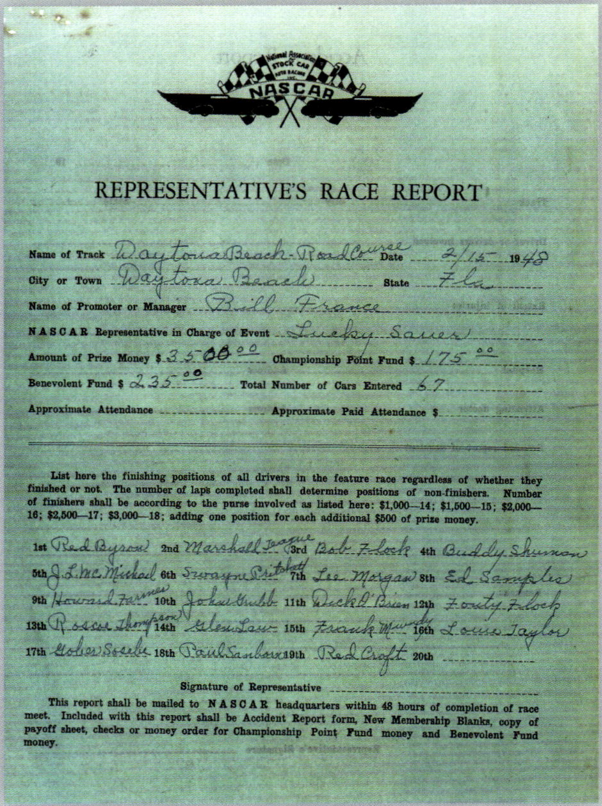

NASCAR

REPRESENTATIVE'S RACE REPORT

Name of Track Daytona Beach-Road Course Date 2/15 1948
City or Town Daytona Beach State Fla
Name of Promoter or Manager Bill France
NASCAR Representative in Charge of Event Lucky Sauer
Amount of Prize Money $ 3500.00 Championship Point Fund $ 175.00
Benevolent Fund $ 235.00 Total Number of Cars Entered 67
Approximate Attendance Approximate Paid Attendance $

List here the finishing positions of all drivers in the feature race regardless of whether they finished or not. The number of laps completed shall determine positions of non-finishers. Number of finishers shall be according to the purse involved as listed here: $1,000—14; $1,500—15; $2,000—16; $2,500—17; $3,000—18; adding one position for each additional $500 of prize money.

1st Red Byron 2nd Marshall Teague 3rd Bob Flock 4th Buddy Shuman
5th J.L. McMichael 6th Swayne Pritchett 7th Lee Morgan 8th Ed Samples
9th Howard Farmer 10th John Grubb 11th Dick O'Brien 12th Fonty Flock
13th Roscoe Thompson 14th Glen Law 15th Frank Mundy 16th Louis Taylor
17th Gober Sosebee 18th Paul Sanborn 19th Red Croft 20th

Signature of Representative

This report shall be mailed to NASCAR headquarters within 48 hours of completion of race meet. Included with this report shall be Accident Report form, New Membership Blanks, copy of payoff sheet, checks or money order for Championship Point Fund money and Benevolent Fund money.

(LEFT) **The original handwritten race results page from NASCAR's debut on February 15, 1948, right down to the rusting staple in the top-left corner.**

(OPPOSITE) **Fonty Flock was a pre-race favorite in NASCAR's first race—until he rolled his 1939 Ford and ended up amid palmetto scrub and sea oats.**

FONTY FLOCK
RA.9412
Al Dykes
1
SERVICE

ROBERT NOLD "RED" BYRON

BESPECTACLED AND BALDING. That was then and now, the two labels seemingly adhered to Red Byron, labels that absolutely belie the badass reality of the World War II veteran who became NASCAR's first champion and then its second, during the 1948 and '49 seasons.

It's the old adage—appearances can be deceiving—at work. History illuminates: Byron, who could've passed for a college professor, was a special man for a special time, saddling right up next to "Big Bill" France himself in that regard.

Byron's racing roots were in pre-war, pre-NASCAR, Southeastern dirt action. His racing excellence was owed to those experiences and, more so, to time in battle. He came home from the war wounded, his left leg withered, but his spirit sturdier than ever. And so, when cars raced on the beach, or one of the short track red-dirt bullrings, comparatively, it simply wasn't that big of a damn deal. What's a little fender rubbin' compared to trying to kill or be killed with democracy in the balance?

Stock car racing? Bring it on. He'd been through worse. More than once, as a flight engineer and tail gunner. The worst of the worst happened on his fifty-eighth and final mission that departed from the Aleutian Islands into the North Pacific. A bomb got hung up in the plane's open bay. Byron climbed down into the bay and wrangled the bomb loose. As it dropped, it exploded. Byron was unprotected.

He survived, somehow, with his left leg in terrible shape due to shrapnel, and amputation seemed almost certain. But an arduous twenty-seven months later, Byron emerged from a military hospital. He was soon behind the wheel of a sedan, aided by a hand-operated clutch. And then, in the fall of 1946, old friends Raymond Parks and Red Vogt came calling to go racing. Again.

Before the war, they'd been hell, the three of 'em. Byron, a Virginia native, had moved to Anniston, Alabama—just down the road from where Talladega Superspeedway now sits—and had started racing with moderate success. He wanted more, so he relocated to Atlanta and started competing at famed Lakewood Speedway. Parks and Vogt, legends in the works as a car owner and mechanic, respectively, knew talent when they saw it. Byron was also adept at turning wrenches himself—always had been since he was a teen. This further boosted his worth as a racer.

A TRIUMVIRATE was born, with a benefit Parks and Vogt could not overlook nor underestimate: In sharp—*sharp*—contrast to most drivers of those days when moonshining and racing went hand in hand, Byron didn't even drink for chrissakes. At all. Factor in his soft-spoken, measured demeanor and an innate intelligence that further separated him from rivals. This guy took reliability to a new level.

"Red Byron was a nice guy with a good soul," not exactly common traits among stock car drivers, writes Neal Thompson in *Driving with the Devil: Southern Moonshine, Detroit Wheels, and the Birth of NASCAR*.

The uncommon triumvirate won races. Lots of them, until the war intervened.

LIFE IS WEIRD. The war ruins Byron's leg. The leg then leads to one of NASCAR's most legendary innovations, the ultimate one-off that became normal equipment: a specially designed clutch pedal bolted to the brace on the leg. Undoubtedly daring, because sketchiness loomed. If Byron's car flipped, rolled, or caught on fire, a leg bolted to the clutch would not be optimum.

That was the setup devised mainly by Vogt for that first reunion run, at long-gone Seminole Speedway near Orlando, Florida, in February 1946. Bill France Sr. promoted the race and drove as well. Byron took the checkered flag.

The setup stuck, sketchiness be damned. In 1948, NASCAR's inaugural season of fifty-eight modified races, Byron won eleven including the new sanctioning body's debut race on the Daytona Beach and Road Course. The next year, NASCAR debuted the Strictly Stock Division; Byron won two of eight events to repeat as NASCAR champ. Years later, then-NASCAR Chairman Bill France Jr. called Byron "the perfect champion."

"Red Byron has always fascinated me," says acclaimed author and ESPN Senior Writer Ryan McGee, who has become a bit of a Byron specialist through the years. McGee wrote a Byron opus in 2012; he reposts it on ESPN.com every year, right around Veterans Day. McGee even used to have an old "Red Byron" Twitter feed, where he would address today's NASCAR from an imagined Byron perspective. Fun stuff, but McGee had a purpose.

"He's the original champion who really should've been dead," McGee adds. "To me, he's the ultimate 'Greatest Generation' guy."

That theory about war being a perfect prep for racing? McGee subscribes.

"And, you know, we make a really big deal out of him strapping his leg to the clutch but I'm thinking . . . well, whatever? If you were stuck on what was supposed to be your death bed for as long as he was . . . and you're going to spend the rest of your life with a leg full of shrapnel . . . to have crawled out there to cut that bomb loose . . . to have flown so many missions in a freaking rattle trap of a plane. If you've done all that, then strapping your foot to the clutch was nothing. You know *he* was like, whatever. Although to us mere mortals, that idea is insane.

"He was so smart, but no formal education. He just figured things out. And in another timeline, he could've been an engineer. He lived this ridiculous life. Like I said, fascinating."

Byron's career detoured after his two NASCAR championship seasons. In 1950, he raced in only four NASCAR events, then five more in 1951, opting to make his own schedules. Bill France Sr. hated that like poison; Byron did not even appear in the final series standings those last two years.

After that, health concerns led Red to quit racing—as a driver. For the rest of his life, he was into sports cars, becoming a mechanic and crew chief for several top teams; when he died due to heart problems at the age of forty-five in 1960, he was operating a Sports Car Club of America team.

Byron was inducted into the NASCAR Hall of Fame in 2018. The Hall's executive director Winston Kelley accepted on Byron's behalf. "One thing is crystal clear [about this induction]," Kelley said that evening. "Red Byron's pioneering spirit, contributions, and accomplishments solidify his legacy—and his rightful place in the NASCAR Hall of Fame."

(continues on page 29)

(ABOVE LEFT) **Bill France Sr. (*center*) with NASCAR's first champion crew chief, Red Vogt (*left*) and first champion driver, Red Byron (*right*).**

(ABOVE RIGHT) **Red Byron finished second in the 1950 Daytona Beach and Road Course race, the last time he contended seriously on the sand.**

(OPPOSITE) **The classic Red Byron, NASCAR's first and forever champion.**

STRICTLY STOCK DEBUT: JUNE 19, 1949

IN RETROSPECT, having to wait an extra season before starting his prized Strictly Stock Division worked out fine for Bill France Sr. The inaugural NASCAR season in 1948 was envisioned as a Strictly Stock showcase but it didn't happen due to wartime production lulls of passenger sedans. Stock cars were scarce; modifieds weren't and so they carried the day in '48. Fifty-two races' worth.

In '49, with production again approaching normal, there were enough cars to forge on with the Strictly Stock concept. In case anyone has forgotten, Bill Sr. considered that concept as central to *anything* NASCAR would do in the future.

The future arrived in real time on June 19, 1949, at Charlotte Speedway, a ¾-mile dirt oval that was less than pristine, with a rough racing surface that would lose a portion of its red clay on every turn, with a spray coating grandstand spectators with each lap as cars pitched sideways coming out of Turn 4. Those in the know knew, back in those days, that you never drank the last sip of beer. It was mostly mud.

The 150-mile race was dubbed the Strictly Stock Car Classic. Crowd estimates varied, partly because of the considerable number of fans who snuck in. Bill France Jr., just two months past his sixteenth birthday but already becoming immersed in the family business, was a member of ad hoc security that day.

"That was a big day for me, for reasons that had nothing to do with racing," Bill Jr. said. "My dad had this great idea that I would spend the day pulling people down off the fences to keep them from getting in without paying. I'd reach up, yank them down, then go on to the next person and do the same thing. A lot of times, I had to take off running to keep from getting my butt whipped because, every now and then, one of the guys I pulled off the fence was a big sonofabitch."

According to most accounts, between fifteen and twenty thousand watched the race, one way or another.

With the stage set, why not roll out an audacious debut that would have it all? Despite competition from the rival National Stock Car Racing Association (NSCRA) having an event the same day in Atlanta, many of the sport's major names competed, including several future NASCAR Hall of Fame inductees. Names such as runner-up Fonty Flock, third-place finisher Red Byron, Lee Petty, Curtis Turner, Buck Baker, and NASCAR's first female Strictly Stock driver, Sara Christian.

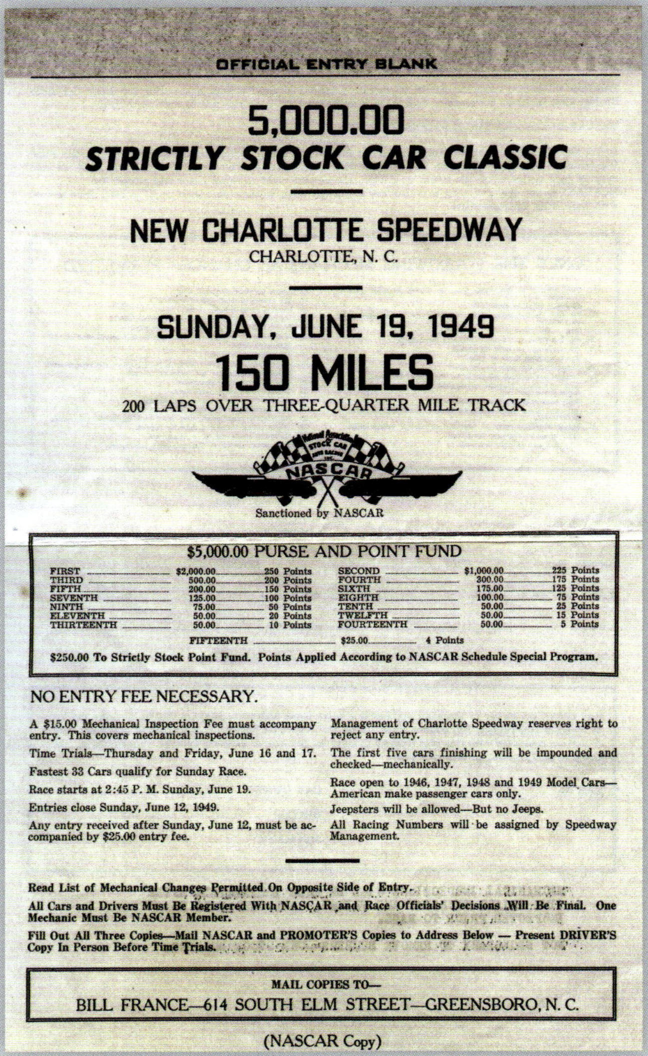

OFFICIAL ENTRY BLANK

5,000.00
STRICTLY STOCK CAR CLASSIC

NEW CHARLOTTE SPEEDWAY
CHARLOTTE, N. C.

SUNDAY, JUNE 19, 1949
150 MILES
200 LAPS OVER THREE-QUARTER MILE TRACK

Sanctioned by NASCAR

$5,000.00 PURSE AND POINT FUND

FIRST	$2,000.00	250 Points	SECOND	$1,000.00	225 Points
THIRD	500.00	200 Points	FOURTH	300.00	175 Points
FIFTH	200.00	150 Points	SIXTH	175.00	125 Points
SEVENTH	125.00	100 Points	EIGHTH	100.00	75 Points
NINTH	75.00	50 Points	TENTH	50.00	25 Points
ELEVENTH	50.00	20 Points	TWELFTH	50.00	15 Points
THIRTEENTH	50.00	10 Points	FOURTEENTH	50.00	5 Points
FIFTEENTH	$25.00	4 Points			

$250.00 To Strictly Stock Point Fund. Points Applied According to NASCAR Schedule Special Program.

NO ENTRY FEE NECESSARY.

A $15.00 Mechanical Inspection Fee must accompany entry. This covers mechanical inspections.

Time Trials—Thursday and Friday, June 16 and 17.

Fastest 33 Cars qualify for Sunday Race.

Race starts at 2:45 P. M. Sunday, June 19.

Entries close Sunday, June 12, 1949.

Any entry received after Sunday, June 12, must be accompanied by $25.00 entry fee.

Management of Charlotte Speedway reserves right to reject any entry.

The first five cars finishing will be impounded and checked—mechanically.

Race open to 1946, 1947, 1948 and 1949 Model Cars—American make passenger cars only.

Jeepsters will be allowed—But no Jeeps.

All Racing Numbers will be assigned by Speedway Management.

Read List of Mechanical Changes Permitted On Opposite Side of Entry.

All Cars and Drivers Must Be Registered With NASCAR and Race Officials' Decisions Will Be Final. One Mechanic Must Be NASCAR Member.

Fill Out All Three Copies—Mail NASCAR and PROMOTER'S Copies to Address Below — Present DRIVER'S Copy In Person Before Time Trials.

MAIL COPIES TO—
BILL FRANCE—614 SOUTH ELM STREET—GREENSBORO, N. C.

(NASCAR Copy)

The official entry blank for the NASCAR Strictly Stock Division's first race. No entry fee necessary! In lieu of that, though, teams paid a $15 "mechanical inspection fee." Pretty creative approach.

Glenn Dunaway, the ultimate forgotten NASCAR man, raced three seasons (1949 through '51) in the NASCAR Cup Series. He never won, but he did finish a solid ninth in the 1949 championship points. He almost won NASCAR's first Strictly Stock event. Wonder how many times he told that story? Dunaway died tragically in 1964 at the age of forty-nine, after his car was struck by a train.

Hubert Westmoreland owned the car that Glenn Dunaway drove to apparent victory in the Strictly Stock Division debut before it was disqualified. Westmoreland sued NASCAR and lost. The what-goes-around footnote: Fifteen months later, a car co-owned by old moonshiner Westmoreland and NASCAR President Bill France Sr. was driven to victory at another new track, Darlington (South Carolina) Raceway, by Johnny Mantz. . . . And don't start with any of that conflict-of-interest stuff . . . or, on second thought, go ahead. Bill Sr. would love the chatter.

Jim Roper won the first Strictly Stock race after Glenn Dunnaway was disqualified—and never won again in NASCAR. Probably explains why we don't have a better picture.

The *Charlotte Observer* called Christian's entry the addition of a "feminine complexion" and reported that she was "anything but afraid." Good to know.

The field of thirty-three also had some entries that oozed good ol' boyness: Slick Smith, Skimp Hersey, Pee Wee Martin. Others named Sterling, Archie, B. E., and Felix.

The cars were stars too with *nine* manufacturers represented: Buick, Cadillac, Chevrolet, Ford, Hudson, Kaiser, Lincoln, Mercury, and Oldsmobile. And the purse: $5,000 total, $2,000 to the winner, and a guarantee of payment! In the 1940s pre-NASCAR, payouts were not always a given. Further incentive was the additional guarantee of a season-long points system that would name a legitimate NASCAR champion at year's end, starting with the Charlotte race.

Glenn Dunaway was ready to accept two grand, thank you very much, but the first-ever post-race Strictly Stock inspection resulted in the first disqualification. Car owner Hubert Westmoreland had altered the '47 Ford's rear springs in the way moonshiners did, to improve handling. Original runner-up Jim Roper, who drove a '49 Lincoln, was handed the victory in what proved to be his only Strictly Stock appearance.

Westmoreland sued NASCAR; the case got tossed by another Carolinian legend—Middle District Court Judge Johnson Jay Hayes. (A footnote: Hayes is buried in North Wilkesboro, North Carolina, 2½ miles from North Wilkesboro Speedway.)

With the NASCAR rule book duly upheld and the debut boosted by surprise post-race publicity, it was time to undoubtedly proclaim the Strictly Stock Division—the forerunner of today's NASCAR Cup Series—open for business. Initial indications supported "Big Bill" France's steadfast belief that race fans most wanted to watch cars that looked like their own.

That first race, then, was an immediate gauntlet. Thrown down on the oil-stained red dirt with the message that rules, by God, were going to be rules this time around. As Lee Petty used to tell people years later regarding NASCAR and the budding authority of "Big Bill": "It's his ball, ball game, and his ball field."

With only one referee.

SARA CHRISTIAN AND LOUISE SMITH

THE IMPORTANCE of true mavericks Sara Christian and Louise Smith to stock car history cannot be overemphasized. Their career NASCAR Cup Series statistics, a combined eighteen starts from 1949 to '52, belie their immense contributions, which started with the simple fact that they were *there*, right in the good ol' thick of things.

The fact that neither came close to winning a Cup Series race matters not at all. Both ran respectably in an environment that had to be—just a guess here—less than 100 percent hospitable, if not downright hostile, at times. "NASCAR is no place for a female driver." Janet Guthrie heard that in the 1970s. So did Danica Patrick in the 2010s. Christian and Smith heard it in the 1940s and, in all likelihood, at a higher volume.

Sara Christian was there first—the only woman in the field of the first NASCAR Strictly Stock race, in June 1949.

SARA CHRISTIAN

Christian became the first female driver in the Strictly Stock Division, the forerunner to the NASCAR Cup Series, by starting thirteenth in the series' debut on June 19, 1949, at the then-new Charlotte Speedway. She drove a '47 Ford owned by her husband, Frank Christian.

Polesitter Bob Flock took over Christian's Ford after his own car had problems and finished fourteenth. Accounts vary, but it sure looks like Frank gave his wife the hook and gave a major star the seat. Makes for a better story, at least.

Christian's next series start came at the Daytona Beach and Road Course in July, the event that would evolve into the Firecracker 400 at Daytona International Speedway. She finished eighteenth in a field of twenty-eight that included Louise Smith and Ethel Flock Mobley. As one might guess, this was the first NASCAR race to have three female drivers. There's more. Christian's husband, Frank, owner of her Ford, drove another one to a sixth-place finish in what ended up as his only NASCAR start.

Christian raced in six of the eight Strictly Stock events held that first season, with a season-best fifth-place finish at Heidelberg Raceway near Pittsburgh, Pennsylvania. That remains the best finish for a female driver in NASCAR Cup Series history. Her thirteenth-place finish in the series championship standings is also a record for women in the Cup Series.

In 1950, she made her only appearance at Hamburg (New York) Speedway, finishing fourteenth. She then retired due to back injuries sustained in a November 1949 crash. "Frank grounded me," she said.

Years after she retired to her native Georgia, Christian maintained that she was treated well—and fairly, for the most part—by her fellow drivers. She considered herself "one of the boys."

"In my opinion, of the women I drove against, Sara was about the best," the old veteran Frank Mundy told the *Richmond Times-Dispatch* in 1993. "She was a damn good driver. If she finished, [when] there were twenty cars in a race, she could finish tenth or twelfth. And with that kind of competition . . . you know how rough we were back in those days."

(RIGHT) **Christian leads a pack of cars at Lakewood Speedway in Atlanta, Georgia, in a '49 non-NASCAR event.**

(BELOW) **Smith's famous wreck—and more-famous post-wreck pose, Occoneechee Speedway, 1947.**

"I always felt like driving a race car was such an unladylike thing," Christian told the *Charlotte Observer* in 1972. "But I liked it. It relaxed me. And back then we had fun. You drove!"

Christian drove again in 1953, a one-off attempt to set a new measured mile (1.6 k) record for Strictly Stock autos. She was one of eleven drivers who beat the previous record of 100.28 mph, zipping down the Atlantic shoreline to the tune of 101.03 mph in a 1952 Oldsmobile.

Christian died in 1980 at the age of sixty-one, in her hometown of Dahlonega, Georgia.

LOUISE SMITH

Louise Smith raced only a few times more (eleven) than Christian in Strictly Stock but achieved far more notoriety. Smith is credited with thirty-eight victories in various types of cars, with twenty-eight victories in modifieds.

Compared to the sometimes-demure Christian, Smith certainly looked and acted more like a race driver. At least that was the opinion of NASCAR great Tim Flock, who told the *Richmond Times-Dispatch*, "Sara was a nice lady . . . Louise was pretty rough. You'd see her walking around those pits like a man . . . she didn't take no shit off nobody."

Veteran journalist and author Deb Williams has written extensively about both Christian and Smith, and she got to know Smith well.

"They were very different women," Williams said. "Louise was a hard drinking . . . crazy woman. Sara was known as a good race car driver. Louise was known more for wrecking than racing."

Smith won races but she won many fans because of her aggressive style—and an epic story or two that resulted.

Here's one.

In 1947, when Smith was racing at Occoneechee Speedway in Hillsborough, North Carolina, a spectacular crash produced a demolished car. Smith climbed out to check the damage, then somehow slid back into the mangled cockpit, bent her head—and smiled wide for photographers. The shot was unique and is now somewhat iconic, portraying Louise Smith as the badass racer she truly was.

And then there was the time . . .

In July 1949, Smith came to Daytona Beach to check out beach-road course action. She came as a *spectator*, the story goes, and she couldn't stand it. The family sedan, a new Ford convertible, became a race car. It then became a ruined race car after Smith crashed and rolled—but still finished twentieth in a twenty-eight-car field.

Her hometown newspaper in Greenville, South Carolina, ran the race wire story, which highlighted Smith's mishap. She returned home on a Greyhound bus, without the Ford, with a flimsy story ready to go about the new car breaking down. She was greeted by Noah Smith, one pissed-off husband, clutching the paper.

Smith retired from race car driving in 1956; the sport lured her back fifteen years later, and she began a run of sponsoring cars, including Ronnie Thomas's Rookie of the Year effort in 1978.

Louise Smith on Daytona Beach before the Sportsman race in 1951.

Smith died in 2006 at the age of eighty-nine. Eleven years later she was reintroduced, as the inspiration for Disney Pixar's *Cars 3* character Louise "Barnstormer" Nash, another maverick, of course.

RAYMOND PARKS

RAYMOND PARKS, it would seem, is all things to all people who consider NASCAR important and, even more so, NASCAR history.

Pioneer multicar team owner. Winner of NASCAR's first two championships. Fielder of first-rate race cars. Ally and financier of NASCAR founder "Big Bill" France during the sport's early years.

But that's not all. Parks must also be remembered as an accomplished moonshine runner, operator of an illegal numbers racket in the Atlanta area, owner of multiple liquor stores, and an impeccable dresser; Gotti goes South—and one of the most intriguing figures in NASCAR history.

In short, the real deal when it comes to assessing, and certainly explaining, NASCAR's origins.

Born in 1914 near Dawsonville, Georgia, Raymond Parks found himself behind bars for three months in 1928 after police caught him running a booze errand for his father. Talk about a precursor. Parks found a new friend while in the can, a veteran shine runner who told Parks to give him a call when he was released. Parks did just that, in all likelihood quickly.

Parks' career moved fast. Another precursor. He added working at his uncle's service station to his shine time. In several years, he had saved enough to buy out his uncle and soon buy a substantial property south of Atlanta, big enough for a family and several moonshine stills. And thus, our man Raymond wasn't completely legit until the 1940s, but he was quite successful. He had doubled down in the '30s, running both liquor stores and shine.

Eventually the legit part stuck, but not before Parks made the natural progression from moonshine running to stock car racing. His cousins, shine runners Lloyd Seay and Roy Hall, recruited Parks—and his money—in 1938. Parks brought in a buddy named Red Vogt to build and maintain the cars that were stickered up to promote Parks' gas station. Occasionally, a guy from Daytona Beach, Florida, named Bill France, would drive for Parks.

And then, in only a few years, it was all done. Seay was shot and killed in a moonshine dispute. Hall was jailed. France quit racing to concentrate on promoting events. And Parks, well, he got drafted.

Post-war, Parks jumped back in, and Hall was with him, out of jail and in the victory lane in September 1945. In December 1947, Parks and Vogt were among the attendees at NASCAR's first organizational meetings. When the four-day gathering concluded, NASCAR was the name and "Big Bill" France was the boss, as the new sanctioning body's first president. Parks would be the money man when he wasn't winning championships.

Before long, what would become the first "NASCAR Super Team" formed, with Parks and Vogt reuniting with one of their pre-war aces, Red Byron. Racing with an improvised clutch setup to cover for a severely wounded left leg, Byron won NASCAR's first two championships in 1948 and '49.

"HE DID IT ALL in racing," says journalist and author Jonathan Ingram, a good friend of Parks in the legend's later years.

"He owned the cars. He had the best drivers. He drove the cars himself."

And paid for it by, well, *you know*.

"If it wasn't on the edge of the law, or against the law, or just pushing the envelope, or just doing it his way, then Raymond wasn't interested," Ingram said. "He was bound and determined to work outside the law and snub his nose at authority. That was his thing.

"All of that is the summary, of his maverick side."

The peerless 1950s lineup fielded by Carl Kiekhaefer is often cited as the template for modern multicar/driver teams. But you might want to cite this: Raymond's race cars were perfect aesthetically and mechanically, the former due to Parks' inherent style, the latter due to Vogt's unmatched expertise. Believe it: At once, Parks was everything NASCAR wanted to leave behind and everything it needed to advance. And we're talking about more than just money, no matter where the hell it came from.

"The soul, the spirit, the guts of NASCAR all sprang from the passion of Parks, long before there was a NASCAR," wrote the great sports journalist Ed Hinton, for ESPN.

When Parks quit full-time racing in 1952, he had thirteen victories as an owner. He blamed his exit on the increasing cost of fielding winning teams in NASCAR. One final precursor.

Parks died in 2010 at the age of ninety-six, seven years before his 2017 NASCAR Hall of Fame induction. His granddaughter, Patricia DeBottey, represented Parks that night, accepting the induction ring after an emotional introduction by Kyle Petty.

DeBottey said her grandfather was a man who lived a large life yet was incredibly low key when asked to explain it all.

"He told me his entire life story in about ten minutes," DeBottey said. "And when I asked him how he got into racing, he answered, 'Well, I got some cars and I started winning.'"

(ABOVE LEFT) **Looking the part: The godfather of NASCAR and the don of Atlanta.**

(ABOVE RIGHT) **The first NASCAR "Super Team"—owner Raymond Parks, crew chief/mechanic Red Vogt, driver Red Byron, 1949.**

(RIGHT) **Parks with the hardware indicative of the skill of his drivers, who were moonshine runners or race drivers—and sometimes both.**

RED VOGT

FOR MORE THAN FOUR DECADES, Louis Jerome "Red" Vogt was synonymous throughout the Southeast with going fast. He became, in the words of noted journalist and author Ed Hinton, "the first great maestro of horsepower" in stock car racing and, originally, moonshine running.

Vogt, a native of Washington, DC—he was a teenage friend of Bill France Sr.—moved to Atlanta in 1927, going to work as a mechanic for bootleggers. Eventually, he opened his own garage, a place now part of stock car lore. It was a fledgling model for today's modern NASCAR race shops.

People who saw the place never forgot it; immaculately kept, with the red-headed, rough-talking Vogt immaculately dressed, always, in all white.

The second great maestro of horsepower, Henry "Smokey" Yunick, said he "was in absolute awe of [Vogt's] knowledge." High praise.

Retrospect makes Vogt's rise to notoriety look downright serendipitous, coinciding with America's increasing fascination with the automobile in the 1930s and '40s. Those who could turn wrenches, making machines sing, were something special, indeed.

Neal Thompson, in his book *Driving with the Devil: Southern Moonshine, Detroit Wheels, and the Birth of NASCAR*, described folks like Vogt as "like a shaman who could reveal, interpret, and manipulate the car's grimy inner secrets . . . a minor deity . . . in the chronology of America's racing history, his timing was perfect."

Vogt's history is dense. He is best known for being part of NASCAR's "First Super Team" consisting of himself, car owner Raymond Parks, and driver Red Byron. They won NASCAR's first race in 1948 and its first two championships in 1948–49, with Byron, a World War II veteran, overcoming a permanently injured left leg via the use of an extended clutch designed by . . . Red Vogt.

It was actually Vogt's second "Super Team" experience. Back in '39, he had begun building badass stockers for Parks and his drivers Lloyd Seay and Roy Hall, cousins who were also experienced shine runners. Between 1939 and '41, they won dozens of races and a few championships too.

NASCAR was years away.

Years later, it's intriguing to imagine NASCAR's early seasons dominated by Seay and Hall—and Vogt.

Didn't happen.

Seay was murdered in 1941—shot through the heart during an argument about moonshine money. Hall went to jail for bank robbery in 1946; out in '49, he went back to racing but suffered career-ending injuries in a September crash.

Vogt's lasting fame is also pinned to the famous NASCAR organizational meeting in December 1947, at the Streamline Hotel. Vogt was one of the men in the proverbial smoke-filled room, the Ebony Lounge on the hotel's top floor. More notably, he was the man who suggested the acronym NASCAR—National Association for Stock Car Auto Racing. That wasn't the first choice. NSCRA (National Stock Car Racing Association) was, but the group quickly switched up because a rival organization in Georgia was using the name. Good thing Vogt was in attendance.

Vogt continued to build cars for Parks until the owner left the sport in 1955. In addition to Byron, Fonty Flock and Curtis Turner drove Vogt-prepared rides during those years. Later, Vogt worked for yet another Super Team, fielded by Carl Kiekhaefer. Estimates vary, with some having Vogt-prepared cars winning close to five hundred races between 1926 and 1968, when he retired.

Vogt died at his home in Daytona Beach in 1991. He was eighty-six.

"He was a crackerjack mechanic," said another, Ray Fox.

"Red is the godfather of all racing mechanics," Smokey Yunick liked to say.

Hard to argue with those assessments.

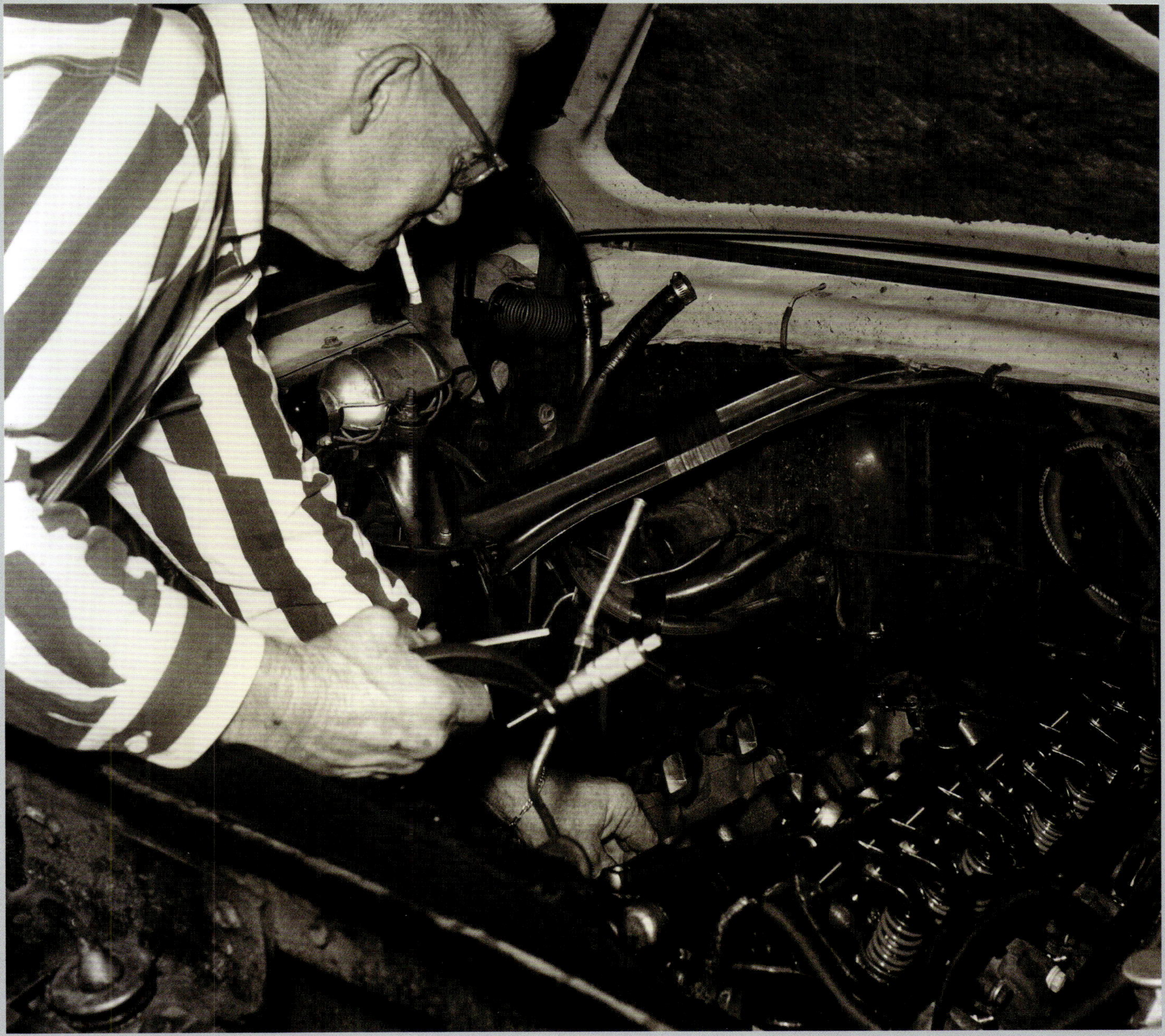

(RIGHT) **Gotta love it: an older Red Vogt turning wrenches with a lit cigarette dangling. Classic.**

(OPPOSITE) **Louis Jerome "Red" Vogt outside his famed Atlanta garage.**

CHAPTER 2

THE 1950s

SUPER CARS, SUPER DRIVERS—AND SUPER SPEEDWAYS

Once it was established, NASCAR grew at near-breakneck speed. After only two years in existence a mile-plus superspeedway was being built in Darlington, South Carolina. This would be the first asphalt-surfaced facility in the sport and, other than the beach course at Daytona and the mile track at Langhorne, Pennsylvania, the only track larger than a ½-mile dirt oval.

IN 1951, WITH THE KOREAN CONFLICT RAGING, the first event held in California made NASCAR a national sport. With the growth of the sport, the auto manufacturers were beginning to take notice. A 250-mile race at Detroit showed the factories how well their products could conduct themselves when put to the ultimate test.

National heroes were beginning to emerge as NASCAR was followed increasingly by the nation's press. And sponsorship by national brands came on board. Names such as Air Lift, Pure Oil Company, Perfect Circle Piston Rings, and Mercury Outboard Motors. The Hudson Motor Company first threw their hat in the ring as a factory sponsor when they gave cars and support to Marshall Teague, a Daytona Beach mechanic and engineer who showed great prowess on the sands of Daytona.

The second half of the 1950s has been called the nation's "happy days" with Eisenhower as president and no major crises to take away the opportunity for the American public to have fun and proceed with their individual interests. New cars were affordable and plentiful, and this played right into NASCAR's hands as their events featured new-model automobiles that the race fan could readily identify with.

CARL KIEKHAEFER

IN THE 1950S, Carl Kiekhaefer built the original multicar powerhouse NASCAR organization. Nothing like it had been seen before. NASCAR's first Super Team built by Raymond Parks in the late 1940s was impressive, but Kiekhaefer took the concept to the max.

Kiekhaefer was a bolt of lightning that flashed briefly across the NASCAR landscape, but still shocked the bejesus out of everyone involved with the sport. Two seasons. That's all it took. But for many in NASCAR, that was enough. Fifty-two victories—including a consecutive run of fifteen—and two Grand National owner championships in 1955–56 with future NASCAR Hall of Famers Tim Flock and Buck Baker at the wheel.

Kiekhaefer's operation, with a lineup of gleaming Chrysler 300s driven by several of NASCAR finest, applied a stranglehold on Bill France Sr.'s show. This deal was new. Revolutionary. Intimidating. Kiekhaefer's cars arrived at dusty racetracks in gleaming haulers. His drivers wore custom-made race suits. Kiekhaefer carried himself with an air of superiority. It was an easy lift.

As you might imagine, Kiekhaefer, an accomplished figure in the world of powerboat engine development and a Yankee no less (Wisconsin), was about as popular as a heart attack in the garage area. He had renowned engineering expertise, a successful business in Kiekhaefer Aeromarine, and in-house corporate sponsorship (Mercury Outboard Motors) for his cars—another NASCAR first.

Toss in an in-house meteorologist present at each race. Atmospheric pressure readings, all that, to aid his cars' setups. Kiekhaefer actually had gasoline cooled before it was pumped into the Chryslers: the cooler the fuel, the more you could squeeze into a tank.

Regarding Kiekhaefer's popularity, it must be noted that he wasn't exactly cozy with anyone—even his drivers and crew members.

"He was a prick," says Buz McKim, longtime NASCAR historian with a master's degree in Kiekhaefer lore. To back up the short, bold opinion, McKim has a story that is at once hilarious and illustrative. Prick or not, Carl Kiekhaefer was serious.

"Kiekhaefer would rent a hotel for a race weekend," McKim said. "He would have all the drivers' rooms on one side of the hotel, and he had all the drivers' significant others in another wing. Then, he would sit in a chair right in the middle of the place near the office, overnight. All night, to make sure nobody got laid. That was because he felt his drivers needed to be one hundred percent, physically. He didn't want them using up their energy."

Whether that old boxing trainer tactic worked, who knows? But one can't help but think that Kiekhaefer's drivers could've partied all night, every night, and it wouldn't have mattered one whit.

If McKim has a master's, Jeffrey Rodengen deserves a doctorate. He authored *the* Kiekhaefer biography, *Iron Fist*, and many other works covering the boating industry such as *The Legend of Mercury*. Rodengen points to rare failures as the catalyst for Kiekhaefer's NASCAR full-court press/success.

NASCAR Grand National Division car owner Carl Kiekhaefer with three of his hot shoes: drivers Herb Thomas, Buck Baker, and Speedy Thompson.

Classic 1950s NASCAR: Two-time champion Buck Baker driving one of Carl Kiekhaefer's powerful Chryslers on the Daytona Beach-Road Course.

In 1951 and '52 Kiekhaefer fielded cars for the legendary Panamericana, the blood, guts, and gasoline affair also known as "the Mexican Road Race," a label that belied its intensity—and danger. Kiekhaefer's entries fared well but they didn't win. Some sort of fuse had been lit. On to NASCAR. And later, upon his exit, Kiekhaefer summed it up this way according to Rodengen: "Make no mistakes, we have no regrets," Kiekhaefer said. "We entered and we left when we wanted to. NASCAR stock racing was one thing when we entered, but it was something entirely different when we left."

Said McKim, "Kiekhaefer came in smoking . . . and he conquered the world."

Why did he leave? Theories abound. Some may be actual reasons, starting with the notion that Bill France Sr. wanted Kiekhaefer gone. NASCAR, indeed, might have applied pressure. After all, he was stinking up "the show."

Drivers and owners, many of them big names in the then-fledgling sport, were starting to stay home on race day. New rules were being written that favored other cars more than the Chryslers. Some of NASCAR's biggest stars forgot where Victory Lane even was; fans hated it.

Kiekhaefer had accomplished what he had sought: dominance and increased visibility for his Mercury Outboards. And so, in 1957, he eased his operation into gear and returned to the world of water. France's exhale could be heard throughout the Southeast. You just had to listen.

(continues on page 44)

Four of Carl Kiehaefer's six cars entered in the February 1956 NASCAR Cup Series race at the Daytona Beach-Road Course take the green flag from starter Frank Swain for a staged publicity photo. From left: Buck Baker (301), Tim Flock (300-A), Frank Mundy (300B), and Speedy Thompson (500-B; number is obscured).

HAROLD BRASINGTON AND DARLINGTON RACEWAY

ALTHOUGH THE BIG TRACKS in Daytona Beach, Florida, and Talladega, Alabama, typically claim the prime billing when it comes to NASCAR's modern superspeedways, the sport's first asphalt superspeedway was built long before those big tracks in an unlikely spot set in the midst of racing superfandom.

The establishment of NASCAR's first asphalt superspeedway in rural Darlington, South Carolina, was the dogged result of South Carolinian Harold Brasington Sr., who did not let the pioneering idea nor the possible resistance to it ever deter his spirit.

Harold Brasington had traveled to the Indianapolis 500 and experienced the atmosphere of a huge racing event. It was something he wanted to replicate back home for the large and emerging stock car racing fanbase. And while Brasington was absolutely certain his vision of a track would be a huge success, he still had to get the funding for his dream.

And if you believe the folklore, that money came from a distracted card game when Brasington brazenly asked and received distracted permission to build his speedway on one side of a property owned by Sherman Ramsey. Called "The Farm" by locals, this tract of land and the speedway were about to become a foundational part of the sport of NASCAR.

Nearly a decade before those traditional high-banked superspeedways in Daytona and Talladega appeared, Brasington began construction on Darlington—a unique construction.

The original 1.25-mile track was famously built around a fish pond and to compensate for the unique spread of land that allowed, Darlington was built with completely different track ends. The first and second turns would have a smaller radius than the third and fourth turns—it was an "egg shape" that is a unique marker of the track still today and makes a driver's mastery of Darlington Raceway rare and appreciated.

So much so that more than twenty-five thousand people—twice what organizers expected and fueled by enthusiastic fans overturning fences—attended the track's 1950 Labor Day weekend debut of (what was then spelled out) the "Southern Five Hundred." And in homage to his experience at the Memorial Day Indianapolis 500 years earlier, Brasington set an 11 a.m. ET green flag.

An incredible seventy-five cars competed but Californian Johnny Mantz turned in a dominant day at the track's debut, leading 351 of the race's 400 laps and easily holding off Fireball Roberts for a 9-lap victory in NASCAR's first ever 500-mile race.

It was the culmination of a nearly year-long construction of a new and innovative racing venue: Its asphalt pavement, 14-degree banking, and varying turn radii made Darlington Raceway a significant addition to the world of racing then. And now.

Harold Brasington, who would also go on to play a major role in the creation of the renowned Charlotte Motor Speedway and North Carolina Motor Speedway in Rockingham, North Carolina, was awarded the NASCAR Hall of Fame Landmark Award in 2016 for his pioneering efforts in the sport.

(ABOVE LEFT) **Harold Brasington opened NASCAR's first superspeedway, the now-legendary Darlington Raceway, in 1950. Egg-shaped, yes, but still super.**

(OPPOSITE) **As the photo shows, there wasn't a whole lot going on around Darlington Raceway when it was being finished in early 1950. The first race would be September's inaugural Southern 500.**

(ABOVE RIGHT) **Now that's what you call a pace car, the block-long Buick Roadmaster Convertible. Pace car driver Enoch Staley is at the wheel alongside Darlington Raceway owner Harold Brasington, ready to roll off at the inaugural Southern 500 on Labor Day in 1950. Riding proud atop the back seat is Loomis Chestnut Colvin, wife of Bob Colvin, the second president of the raceway.**

Curtis Turner, NASCAR's first "matinee idol," enjoyed his greatest success in NASCAR's Convertible Division. A post-war stance: race hard, party harder.

CURTIS TURNER

CURTIS TURNER, marching to the beat of his own moonshine-influenced hepcat drummer, was NASCAR's first real "character" to connect with the masses. With plenty of talent and more-than-plenty of personality—*race hard, play harde*—Turner was a model for future fan favorites Fireball Roberts and Fred Lorenzen and any other NASCAR driver who either looked like a movie star or simply wanted to raise hell and be loved for doing so.

Along the way, he acquired the ultimate nickname: "The Babe Ruth of Stock Car Racing." And then he kept it. Literally. The words are on his grave in Roanoke, Virginia, near his hometown of Floyd.

"A giant even among the larger-than-life characters of NASCAR's early years," wrote *Sport Illustrated*'s Richard O'Brien in 2005, reviewing the definitive book about Turner, *Full Throttle: The Life and Fast Times of NASCAR Legend Curtis Turner* by Robert Edelstein. The review came twenty-seven years after Turner was the first NASCAR driver to appear on a *Sports Illustrated* cover. That's correct. NASCAR existed for more than twenty years before the nation's most prestigious sports magazine adequately noticed. *SI* even offered a new nickname in the form of the headline "King of the Wild Road" despite Turner never having won a NASCAR championship.

What a loss for readers, the stick-and-ball commitment by sports journalists of those times. So much material, ignored. NASCAR drivers, especially from the early years, come with seemingly never-ending tales illustrating their lives, ranging from the colorful to the outlandish to the illegal. Bottom line: good copy.

In some cases, tales have obscured talents, like with our man Curtis Turner. There is perhaps no NASCAR driver whose accomplishments have been more overlooked in favor of the *wildness*. Bottom line: more fun to talk about.

With Turner, the tales go back to when he started driving at the age of nine, no big deal up around Floyd in those days. A few years later, the angst of puberty likely didn't bother Turner as it did other boys, since he was already hauling shine by then. Inadvertently, he was also planning for his future. Outrunning the lawman aided development of a take-no-prisoners stock car style.

Pre-NASCAR, Turner and others earned their chops on dirt tracks throughout the Southeast. Unofficial records credit him with hundreds of bullring triumphs. In NASCAR, Turner won seventeen times in the Cup Series. His best Cup season was his second: four victories and fifth place in the final championship standings. His best NASCAR season was in '56, with twenty-two victories and a second-place points finish in the short-lived Convertible Division. Tops down. Figures. Wind in the face and all that.

If the stats look lean, too bad. Turner was named one of NASCAR's Fifty Greatest Drivers in 1998. History's light, however, indeed, shines more on the offtrack side of his life. Writes Edelstein: "He had too much energy knocking around inside him." And so, more than the wins, the imagery is of a NASCAR party animal—with an extra dangerous element.

Turner was an avid pilot who had no problem partying in the air. The classic story is of him landing his plane on a small country road near a liquor store, jumping out of the cockpit, dashing over to the store, returning with a bottle,

Driver Curtis Turner and NASCAR President Bill France Sr. co-drove a Nash in the La Carrera Panamericana road race, a nine-stage, six-day race across Mexico. The race was nearly 2,100 miles long; Turner and France crashed out.

and immediately taking off again. Our runner-up tale: He and fellow driver Joe Weatherly piloting small planes, playing "tag" by touching each other's wings in flight. There had to be a bottle of something under their seats—or between their legs. Quick nip.

When he wasn't winning races or making friends in low places, Turner tried to fill an entrepreneurial leaning that had to start when he saw older folks making so much money from liquor. He lost his ass more than once on business ventures. On the other hand, he did co-found Charlotte Motor Speedway. If you had a third hand, the subject would be the speedway going bankrupt almost immediately. The Teamsters saved the day financially, with an eye toward unionizing NASCAR. Turner got knee-deep in those plans, leading to a four-year NASCAR ban courtesy of "Big Bill" France.

Talking to Edelstein nearly two decades after Full Throttle was published, you would think he was still on the first chapter; his enthusiasm is that fresh. He considers the "maverick" label okay, but he likes his own label better. We can give him that.

"The word 'maverick' is convenient because there were generations of people in NASCAR like Curtis, and certainly like Smokey Yunick, who really defined the word," Edelstein said. "But the word, to me, that really defined Curtis and the word I landed on was 'audacity.' He just did things because he could. It was [being compelled by] the force of being Curtis Turner. And you know, he didn't need to dress the part. He didn't need to act the part. He *was* the part."

The curtain fell on NASCAR's former leading man on October 4, 1970, when the plane he was piloting slammed into a hill in Punxsutawney, Pennsylvania. The town's famed groundhog weather forecasting appearance by Punxsutawney Phil was still four months away.

For NASCAR fans, Phil's expertise was irrelevant: Winter had already arrived. Turner was forty-six years old.

(continues on page 48)

NASCAR CONVERTIBLE DIVISION

THE WILDEST THING to remember about NASCAR's late-1950s Convertible Division is that those boys rolled at 2.5-mile Daytona International Speedway, in the biggest stock car race in the world.

At the inaugural Daytona 500 in 1959, twenty of the fifty-nine cars hammering away on the high banks were convertibles. NASCAR even held a separate qualifying race for the ragtops. Years later, with safety initiatives front and center, this seems outlandish. Fair enough. But it was really something, ill-advised or not.

As was the whole four-year lifespan of the Convertible Division. From 1956 to '59, 117 races were run with the tops down, fulfilling a goal of Bill France Sr. to schedule more events at more tracks. Demand for NASCAR racin' was growing exponentially. In the convertibles, he had a spectacle: Fans being able to see the drivers in the cockpits, that was the hook.

The convertibles became a fan favorite as the drivers were fully exposed to the crowd, who loved to watch the racers work the steering wheel, especially on dirt tracks. Shown here dueling at Asheville-Weaverville Speedway is Curtis Turner (26) and Bob Welborn (49).

In 1955, NASCAR announced a merger with a convertible series from the Society of Auto Sports, Fellowship, and Education, based in Indianapolis. The acronym "SAFE" seems weird considering the competitive environment, but whatever. Times were different.

Historian Greg Fielden, in his book *Rumblin' Ragtops*, writes that Bill France had an intertest in convertibles, "But he didn't want to start from square one."

"Coming at a time when our plans for a superspeedway in Daytona Beach [the future Daytona International Speedway] are rapidly jelling, I believe this move will have considerable bearing on making Daytona Beach the real speed capital of the world," France told *National Speed Sport News* in 1956. Side note: *Take that, Indianapolis.*

The former convertible series was called the Circuit of Champions. Not all those champions chose to race under NASCAR sanctioning, perhaps because they'd be facing hot shoes like Curtis Turner.

In '56, Turner came to convertibles and brought an ass kickin' with him, winning twenty-two of the forty-two races he entered in a forty-seven-race season, although super-consistent Bob Welborn won the first of three consecutive division titles. Former SAFE drivers won only twice.

Turner's first victory came in the Division's debut on the Daytona Beach and Road Course. The next season, Turner won eleven more times.

Safety concerns, wavering factory support of teams, and dwindling interest by the sport's major drivers slowly led to the division's shutdown after the '59 season, but not before a kid named Richard Petty won his first NASCAR race of any type. Petty ended his career with one convertible victory and two hundred in the NASCAR Cup Series.

The convertibles didn't completely vanish after 1959. Several tracks continued to run one-off convertible events into the early 1960s, most notably Darlington Raceway. The track had a convertible race on Memorial Day until 1962 which—get this—awarded full points for NASCAR's premier Grand National Division.

NASCAR convertibles, gone but not forgotten as the adage goes. That's not likely to change. As promoter extraordinaire Humpy Wheeler said, "It was one of the most entertaining things that racing has ever had."

Playin' Possum: It was anything but, at this moment on February 17, 1957, on the Daytona Beach and Road Course. Lewis "Possum" Jones, in the number 48, duels legendary Lee Petty in the NASCAR Convertible Series race on the sand.

Frank Mundy (No. 503) and Bob Welborn launch from the front row at the start of the April 22, 1956, Convertible Series race at Hickory Speedway in Newton, North Carolina. They are trailed by Marvin Panch (No. 98), Curtis Turner (No. 26), Gene Blair (No. 90), and Joe Weatherly (No. 12). Welborn would go on to win the race.

Two-time NASCAR Cup Series champion Tim Flock and his racing siblings, Ethel Flock Mobley and Fonty Flock.

THE FLOCKS

IF PERSONALITY and intrigue alone won NASCAR championships, the Flock family would be one historical dynasty. They are, in fact, an important part of the sport's timeline—this pioneering family of speed—as good on the race course as they were interesting off it.

Among the eye-raising antics of this Alabama racing family was a brother, Tim Flocko, who famously competed with a monkey "Jocko Flocko" in his race car. In 1949, sister Ethel Flock Mobley joined her brothers—Tim, Bob, and Fonty—to compete at the Daytona Beach and Road Course, marking the first time a NASCAR race included four siblings. And, of note, Ethel beat two of her more experienced brothers that day.

As with many of racing's early stock car heroes, the Flock family was allegedly involved with the booming moonshine business; like several other soon-to-be-racing drivers, they got their racing legs in the bootlegger scene, blazing backwoods roads in the Southeast. And as also often happened, it turned out to be a prime practice opportunity, laps of a different clock.

You could argue the family's unique presence was none too surprising considering that the patriarch of the Flock family, Carl Flock, made his living as a bicycle racer and tightrope walker. Although he died at only fifty-five years old, most of his eight surviving children followed in his unconventional footsteps—from airplane wing walkers to bootleggers to NASCAR's earliest racing stars.

Brothers Bob and Fonty Flock were the first to give stock car racing a try—in a pair of Ford Coupes widely believed to be the same cars the brothers used during the week in their successful bootlegging business. Although they didn't win their first race, they sure caught the racing bug.

By 1948, the three brothers were all in on Bill France's newly introduced National Association for Stock Car Auto Racing (NASCAR); all three won races and finished among the top ten in that very first championship season led by the youngest brother, Tim, who claimed an amazing fifteen race trophies that year.

There was as much personality as racing talent in this family, and even in those early days the Flocks had been bestowed nicknames such as the "Mad Flocks," "The Flying Flocks," and the "Fabulous Flocks." And all three titles fit these brothers and sister well.

Their time as regular competitors in NASCAR's pioneering days created an unexpected type of intrigue. Not only was this a case of good-natured sibling rivalry among the Flocks—Bob, Fonty, Tim, and Ethel—but they were absolutely high-wattage competitors in the sport. Their life backstories as interesting as the front-page stories they earned winning in stock cars.

In fact, four years after Tim made his first official NASCAR start, he raced with that monkey in his car—"Jocko Flocko," who had his own driver's suit. Although it was initially only a publicity stunt, in May 1953, Tim and Jocko won a NASCAR race at Hickory, North Carolina, making Jocko the only winning monkey in NASCAR history.

Unfortunately, a couple weeks later, there was an issue with Flock's car and the monkey put himself in a dangerous situation causing Flock to have to pit late in the race. The monkey was safely removed from the car and Flock sent back out to the track, but it cost him a prime finishing position. And that was the end of Jocko's racing career.

(ABOVE LEFT) **Bob Flock, one of the four racing Flock family siblings, is a bit overlooked all these years later. Shouldn't be. He won four NASCAR Cup Series races in seven years (1949–1956), finishing second in the series championship in 1949.**

(ABOVE RIGHT) **Two-time NASCAR Cup Series champion Tim Flock actually raced with a pet monkey—Jocko Flocko—in his car briefly during the 1953 season as a clearly weird publicity stunt. That ended after the monkey went apeshit in the car late in one race and could've caused an accident. Moving forward, it was back to the cage for Jocko.**

(LEFT) **The always dapper Fonty Flock before the NASCAR Cup race at Raleigh Speedway in May 1953 with the Frank Christian-owned Red Vogt special Hudson Hornet.**

As Flock told reporters, "I had to get that monkey off my back."

Fortunately for the sport, the Flock brothers still had plenty of racing to do as bona fide stars in NASCAR.

Fonty Flock won nineteen NASCAR Grand National races and finished top five in the championships four times. One of his most memorable winning efforts was the 1952 Southern 500 at Darlington (South Carolina) Raceway—a race he won wearing a vacation-type Bermuda shirt and argyle socks.

Tim Flock would go on to earn NASCAR's 1952 and 1955 Grand National titles—driving an iconic Hudson Hornet in that '52 triumph. In all, he claimed thirty-nine pole positions and thirty-nine race trophies in 189 starts (including that one victory with the monkey co-pilot), and his winning percentage of 21 percent remains among the sport's all-time best. In fact, his eighteen wins in the 1955 season stood as a record for twelve years until Richard Petty exceeded it with twenty-seven wins in 1967.

Tim Flock was inducted into the NASCAR Hall of Fame in 2014—both a personal honor and one he proudly shared with his high-profile pioneering family of speed and bravado.

(RIGHT) **Tim Flock drove immaculately-prepared Chryslers for owner Carl Kiekhaefer in 1955 and '56, winning the NASCAR Cup title in '55.**

(OPPOSITE) **The three racing Flock brothers of NASCAR (from left): Two-time champion Fonty, Tim, and Bob. Their father Carl (far right) was a championship speedboat racer. Two other racing Flocks are missing from this late 1950s shot: Ethel Flock Mobley . . . and Tim's co-driving simian, Jocko Flocko.**

(ABOVE) **Smokey Yunick leans in to discuss race strategy with driver Paul Goldsmith. The two combined forces to win the final Daytona Beach and Road Course race in 1958.**

(OPPOSITE) **Henry "Smokey" Yunick was either NASCAR's greatest innovator or NASCAR's greatest cheater. A brilliant man—and a NASCAR antagonist—either way.**

SMOKEY YUNICK

OKAY, FOLKS, here it is. The story you've been looking for first while ignoring the other chapters—we hope temporarily—because, by God, you gotta find out what more there is to read about the gentleman who personifies the word "maverick" more than any SOB in the history of NASCAR.

Ends up, there's still quite a bit left to both read and ponder about Henry "Smokey" Yunick, a man who was a pilot in World War II, was part of Daytona 500 and Indianapolis 500 championship efforts, two Cup Series crew chief championships, and held the unofficial title of biggest pain in the ass to NASCAR for many years.

Let's start with the main staple of the Yunick legend. Did he cheat? Or did he just squeeze the NASCAR rule book like a sponge, getting every drop out of every opening he could find? Ambiguity was Smokey's ally. When he looked at that too-small-for-anyone type in the too-big-for-him NASCAR rule book, he saw a loophole in every line.

"I really just read the rule book carefully," he said in a televised interview with SPEED. "If a nut, bolt, or part wasn't specifically mentioned, or a measurement wasn't given, I assumed those items were 'fair game' . . . as a result of my reading of the rules, I think that by 1970, one-half of the technical rules section of a NASCAR rule book was dedicated to me. Quite an honor actually."

The Yunick legacy in NASCAR is two-tiered.

On one tier lie the many rule-bending ideas he brought to the NASCAR inspection area: an 11-foot (3.3 m) extended fuel line woven through the race car . . . the use of nitrous oxide for qualifying run boosts . . . putting an inflated basketball in the fuel tank and, after inspection, deflating the ball, yanking it out, and refilling the tank . . . lighter-than-normal window glass, to cut weight . . . a Chevrolet Chevelle built to seven-eighths scale . . . cooling gasoline before putting it into the race car so the gas would expand during a race, increasing fuel mileage.

Things like that, accented by a huge dislike for the way Bill France Sr. and, later, his son Bill Jr., ran NASCAR. The feeling, we can virtually guarantee, was mutual. (Yunick made this public knowledge in his three-volume autobiography entitled *Best Damn Garage in Town: The World According to Smokey.*)

SMOKEY'S
"BEST DAMN GARAGE IN TOWN"
Daytona Beach
MECHANICS–
JUNIOR ROBBINS
FRANK CANNON
HARRY VAN DRIEL

Attention to detail: very important when you're trying to fool NASCAR officials. Especially if your name was Smokey Yunick.

The other tier is all respectability and much more important than any attempts to win a race. Smokey, you see, was all about safety, especially after the death of his friend Fireball Roberts in 1964 after a fiery crash. He built an early version of today's SAFER barrier (soft walls) using plywood and tires . . . he invented the fuel bladder concept . . . he had nine racing-related patents approved between 1978 and 1996.

"There were a lot of other people who were very creative about reading the rulebook in those days," said Tom Jensen, Curatorial Affairs Manager at the NASCAR Hall of Fame and author of *Cheating: An Inside Look at the Bad Things Good NASCAR Winston Cup Racers Do in Pursuit of Speed.*

"The rule book was much smaller and it left a lot of room for interpretation. So a lot of what Smokey did and others did was try to read the rule book and read between the lines.

"He was an incredible mind. He was also a bit of a social miscreant, I think. Somebody who certainly had his share of run-ins with the France family and with NASCAR inspectors. But there's no question he was one of the great minds [in NASCAR]."

Yunick became a folk hero among NASCAR fans. He left the sport in 1970 but he never really left, as the legend grew. Smokey remained in Daytona Beach, operating his legendary "Best Damn Garage in Town." He died after a battle with leukemia in 2001, at the age of seventy-seven.

Smokey's daughter, Trish Yunick, interviewed for this book, doesn't remember much about Smokey's years in NASCAR because he was gone all the time. Dad wasn't home. Always at work. Crazy hours. That was a child's bottom line.

As an adult, Trish experienced the legend firsthand and what it meant to so many people, for so many years.

"We had no context as kids, since we never went to the racetrack," Trish Yunick said in a 2024 interview. "And we were very rarely in the race shop.

"Later on, as a young adult, my business at the time was exotic birds, and I was ordering supplies from a company in Washington state. I got to spelling my name. When I got to 'Y U N', the guy on the other end of the phone just had a fit, and he's like, 'Oh, my God, Daytona Beach? Are you related to Smokey?' That was the beginning of my understanding just who Smokey was, in [the public consciousness]."

Trish later moved the birds into a new shop, an extension Smokey built onto his already-legendary garage. She remembers fans riding by constantly, looking out their windows, pointing at the garage, snapping photos. Smokey noticed, and suggested Trish have some Smokey T-shirts made to sell to the gawkers. Big hit.

"That was when I really learned who Smokey was to the fans, from fans who would come in and tell me stories about him," Trish said. And buy tees.

She took the shirts to the SEMA show in Las Vegas, selling them out of the trunk of a car. Bigger hit.

"That's when I learned what Smokey meant to the industry," Trish said.

It was a rogue move, not allowed at SEMA. Nobody said a word. Smokey would've loved it. Maverick action.

Trish Yunick wants other people to learn what it took her years to absorb. And she wants that to lead to a NASCAR Hall of Fame induction. The animated character in *Cars 3* named and patterned after Smokey isn't enough, folks.

Ken Willis, longtime columnist for NASCAR's hometown paper, the *Daytona Beach News-Journal*, got to know Smokey well, thanks to regular visits to the garage. He's thumbs-up for induction, mainly because of innovations Smokey devised "and then the wins," Willis added. "He had some big wins."

A grassroots campaign, complete with buttons that read SMOKEY BELONGS has been active since 2023. Trish and many people think an unspoken ban exists, because of her father's disagreements with Bill Sr. and Bill Jr., both deceased.

But talk to NASCAR Chairman and CEO Jim France, Big Bill's youngest son, and he'll tell you there is no blockade. At least not on his part.

"There are a lot of people who deserve to be in the Hall of Fame, and probably will be one day. I would put Smokey in with a lot of them," France said, adding a caveat that is worth pondering: "The relationship between my family and Smokey's family extended beyond my father and brother—and in a good way."

"Smokey was one of those guys that you couldn't make up," Jensen said. "And in the last few years of his life, you'd see him in the garage [at Daytona] and he had those white coveralls [from the old days] on, plus the Stetson hat and the pipe.

"He looked like a ghost, an apparition that had appeared."

(continues on page 56)

ED OTTO

UP FRONT, LET'S CLEAR THE AIR: Ed Otto was essential to NASCAR's early growth. If someone tells you different, they're misinformed.

This just in: an addendum. NASCAR's early growth would have proceeded just fine, thank you, without Ed Otto.

The truth, as they say, likely lies somewhere in the middle.

Sides have been taken in recent years, a line drawn in the sand on the Daytona Beach and Road Course. Well, there would've been a line, if the course still existed.

Ed Otto, generally considered Bill France Sr.'s right-hand man at the outset of NASCAR's existence, left the sanctioning body in 1963. The exit was a tad acrimonious publicly, probably more so behind the scenes.

Here's the tragedy: History had already sold Otto short, but that's due, in part, to NASCAR's relative lack of popularity during its first few decades when compared to other sports. Latent ill will—then and now—serves only to obscure Otto's immense contributions, especially among casual or newbie fans.

Otto, Pat Purcell, Bill Tuthill, and Louis Ossinsky formed NASCAR's first "cabinet." All had twenty percent interest in NASCAR "stock," which may have been a bit fictitious in the late 1940s.

Otto, the fedora-wearing New Jersey "Yankee," emerged as a public face of the organization, running second only to France. Like the boss, Otto was a promoter, first and foremost—one of the greatest in auto racing history. And that preceded NASCAR.

Otto was well known in racing circles beyond the Southeast, and just what NASCAR needed, according to Otto's son Edgar, writing in the book, *Ed Otto: NASCAR's Silent Partner.* "It was Ed Otto's job to break the Dixie barrier. It would be his schmoozing skills that would bring in the boys from the North and West. And it would be his responsibility to bring in the new blood needed to keep NASCAR alive and make it a national association. . . . Ed Otto hit the ground running and began spreading the word, preaching the gospel of NASCAR."

He did it, helping to increase the number of NASCAR events outside the Southeast dramatically. He preached until 1963, when a disagreement led to France asking Otto to depart. He did. He got a quarter-million dollars for his forty percent of NASCAR stock, which by then had real value.

As for the theory that NASCAR forgot about Otto after that, it doesn't really hold up. Bill France Jr. wrote a personal letter of recommendation to the National Motorsports Press Association, supporting Otto's induction into the NMPA Hall of Fame. Brian France, during his time as NASCAR chairman and CEO, regularly cited people such as Otto and Purcell when talking about NASCAR history.

Somewhere in the middle . . .

Otto continued to promote races until the 1970s. The lasting image of Otto is him presenting a winner's trophy in some short track Victory Lane, impeccably dressed.

It is a good image.

Ed Otto, NASCAR's first vice president and original right-hand man to NASCAR founder Bill France Sr. He brought promotional expertise that was essential to NASCAR defining itself as a viable sanctioning body.

(OPPOSITE) **Marshall Teague won the NASCAR Cup Series race on Daytona Beach in 1951 in his Hudson Hornet. The Hudson factory noted the attention Teague's victory drew and within a few weeks he was backed by the manufacturer.**

VINCE PIGGINS AND THE HUDSON HORNET

LONG BEFORE the *Cars* animated movie franchise, the Fabulous Hudson Hornet really was, well, fabulous. Those movies—as of 2024, there had been three of them—introduced the first NASCAR "Super Car" to a new audience, many of them children who may well have thought Lightning McQueen was a real driver. Which is cool. It's also cool to know that the Hudson Hornet, driven by an assortment of big-name drivers, was early rocket fuel for "Big Bill" France's promotional aspirations.

Like other significant "mile markers" in NASCAR's early history, the Hornets were not a happening for very long. But when they were on the scene, they would sting you. The Hudson helped NASCAR lift off in the public consciousness with four consecutive championships from 1951 through 1953, the run beginning in NASCAR's fourth season, establishing both machine and men as fan favorites. Herb Thomas was NASCAR's Grand National driver champion in 1951 and '53, sandwiching Tim Flock's title. In '54, Thomas won an owner championship fielding Hudsons. Legendary rule stretcher Smokey Yunick was the champion crew chief in 1951 and '54.

Hudson, founded in 1909, had evolved into a manufacturer popular among working class folks, especially after World War II. You know, NASCAR fans. That inherent cachet was worth even more on the racetrack because Hornets were badass automobiles, starting with imposing, sleek bodywork. Underneath was an inline six-cylinder with two carburetors. Power was balanced by a low center of gravity via a "step down" floor; the floor pan was in line with the chassis frame rails. Handling was superb. "The only real hug-the-road ride" Hudson ads proclaimed, along with "low, wide, and handsome." Women in evening dresses were often part of the ads. Remember, different time.

Call the Hornet another template. Not regarding its mechanics, but its attraction to spectators. In coming years, NASCAR fans would attach themselves to other cars that would become iconic: the Plymouths of the 1960s, Thunderbirds of the '80s, Monte Carlos of the '90s. The fervor in those later decades was real, and essential to NASCAR's connection with ticket buyers.

Way back when, Hudson's brass thought it was essential. The manufacturer was the first to use the "win on Sunday, sell on Monday" slogan to boost its connection with NASCAR.

Vince Piggins, at 6 foot 4 (1 m 90 cm), almost as tall as "Big Bill" France, was considered the "father" of the Hudson and also served as the catalyst in Hudson's NASCAR success before leaving the company for Chevrolet, where he led development of the Camaro. Nice résumé. Piggins and Hudson's most well-known driver, Marshall Teague—also NASCAR's first treasurer—fine-tuned the engines for NASCAR racing.

In Hudson's 1951 debut, Teague won at the Daytona Beach and Road Course, afterward telling the press that Hudson "is the best automobile on the road today." Smart interview. A year later, he had a groundbreaking personal deal with Hudson.

A Piggins footnote: Pre-Camaro, in 1957, he led the project resulting in famed "Black Widow" Chevys. Buck Baker won the NASCAR championship driving one. He and two others combined for sixteen victories that season.

MARSHALL TEAGUE
FABULOUS HUDSON
HORNET
6

Richard Petty (looking a lot like comedian Adam Sandler) celebrated his first Daytona 500 triumph in 1964.

THE PETTY FAMILY

IT WOULD NOT BE an overstatement to insist that no other major American sport's history—not football, baseball, basketball, or hockey even—could so easily be traced to one single family of competitors. NASCAR's beginnings alone; its glory days, its most precious records, and its place in the everyday competitive lexicon belong in so many ways to the Petty family.

The Pettys have each been NASCAR mavericks in their own way and need.

While so many are instantly familiar with NASCAR Hall of Famer Richard Petty, the winningest driver in NASCAR history with two hundred victories, it was, indeed, his father, Lee Petty, who set the initial mark of achievement—not only for his family but also for the sport at large. And if there was a pioneer maverick in this sport, Lee Petty would fill the bill.

Even considering all the excellence and fame belonging to this generation's Petty namesake, Richard Petty, he got the talent honestly from his father, and it has passed along honestly to two future generations, his son Kyle and late grandson Adam. Another fourth-generation Petty, Thad Moffitt, is still competing in NASCAR today.

Lee Petty, who didn't even start racing until his mid-thirties, absolutely established the path and notoriety for his family. Beginning a professional racing career at thirty-five years old is unheard of now and simply amazing considering all the season championships (1954, '58, and '59) and major race trophies that came later.

But the Petty name was to be a difference maker in some of the sport's most historic ways.

The storyline created by Lee Petty in the 1959 Inaugural Daytona 500, alone, remains an important part of the folklore. Petty had to wait three days before he was officially declared the race winner. He and rival Johnny Beauchamp crossed the finish line side-by-side, but it took multiple photographic and scoring reviews by NASCAR President Bill France Sr. before Petty would officially receive that historic Daytona trophy.

Only three years later, during the famed February Daytona Speedweeks, Lee Petty's full-time career essentially came to an end. While racing hard with Beauchamp—again—during one of the Daytona 500 qualifying races, the two drivers' cars collided and both went over the speedway walls and landed completely outside of the race track—that photograph, now synonymous with the speedway and the sport's most historic chapters.

Petty suffered massive injuries and was hospitalized for more than four months, yet after recovering, he still raced from time to time all the way up until 1964.

By that point, Lee's son Richard was already turning heads and upending expectations competing with his father and, ultimately, turning in the early work of what would be historic proportions . . . making that "Petty Blue" on the family cars a forever-iconic color for NASCAR. Typically dressed offtrack in a showy, personalized cowboy hat with dark sunglasses . . . and a perpetual smile, Richard Petty absolutely lived up to his nickname "The King" and helped foster generations of stock car fans.

Richard Petty earned his unprecedented and forever-unmatched two-hundredth win on a July 4, 1984, summer afternoon at Daytona International Speedway after a starting command delivered by United States President Ronald Reagan. The photograph of Reagan's jet flying away from the

Richard Petty and his iconic No. 43 at Daytona International Speedway, February 1973, at the start of his seventh, and final, championship season.

airport adjacent to the track just as the race started is iconic. Considering the day's events and their multi-historical significance, it was both the perfect launch and the final exclamation point. Such is the Petty legacy.

A twenty-year-old Richard Petty started NASCAR racing in 1958, the year his dad, Lee, won his second championship.

And while we talk a lot about the two-hundredth win, Richard scored the first of his historic victories only two seasons after his first green flag—at the ½-mile Southern States Fairground dirt track in Charlotte, North Carolina. His father, Lee, started from pole position that day but had a mechanical issue, relegating him to twentieth in the twenty-one-car field—an interesting juxtaposition for dad and son with the generational exchange on the horizon.

The legend of Richard Petty's was all go. He set a single-season win mark at twenty-seven victories in 1967—a record that, like so many of his, will never be broken. He topped that amazing twenty-win mark again with twenty-one wins in 1971. He won at least ten races in eight seasons. He earned multiple wins in eighteen consecutive seasons from 1960 through '77.

(LEFT) **Maurice Petty, Richard Petty's brother, was his engine builder for his championship seasons.**

(CENTER) **Dale Inman, Richard Petty's longtime crew chief—and his cousin.**

(RIGHT) **Richard Petty's son Kyle won eight NASCAR Cup Series races during his career.**

Daytona was already a venue synonymous with this first family of speed. And Richard Petty's seven Daytona 500 wins are highly unlikely to be repeated. His two hundred NASCAR Cup Series victories—the last coming that very July afternoon with President Reagan delivering the starting command—will never be equaled. His seven championships is still the high mark decades after he hung up his driving shoes. Only two others, the late great Dale Earnhardt and the generational talent Jimmie Johnson, matched that seven-trophy work of excellence.

Yet, importantly, during all those winning seasons, Petty was considered a gentlemen's driver—full of skill, judgment, and drive that differentiated him both from his contemporaries in the sport's early days and, ultimately, to some degree, the modern era of competitors. The maverick in his case was more about taking the baton from his pioneering dad—and carrying it to heights never seen.

As Richard Petty was able to contend with his father, so too that carried on to the third generation Petty star, Richard's son Kyle. The two raced against each other for fourteen seasons before Richard retired in 1992.

Ironically, Kyle Petty claimed one of his most significant feats, at the very next race, the 1993 season-opening Daytona 500 pole position. In Kyle's thirty-year career of statistics, he won eight races—including wins in four consecutive seasons from 1990 to '93—but his tenure behind the wheel ended in what was becoming a very different and more progressive NASCAR than his father and grandfather experienced.

The sport was now more a part of the American lexicon, with NASCAR races from coast to coast, and a large, eager, and excited fandom awaiting everywhere the circuit traveled. Network television was paying attention and so were the country's corporate bigwigs who would ultimately begin backing both the sport and teams in the garage.

As Kyle Petty closed his driving log, he showed that he also had talent out of the car and on television—announcing and commenting on races, something he still does today. And that variation on the family racing log seemed perfectly timed.

There was, after all, yet another Petty generation on deck and ready to thrill. Kyle's son Adam Petty was popular, respectful, a student of the sport; his youth and obvious talent had the garage buzzing. After racing in the lower levels to get a proper competitive upbringing, Adam stepped up to NASCAR's national series level as a seventeen-year-old competing in what is now known as the Xfinity Series. He started eleventh and finished twenty-seventh in that first race at Gateway International Raceway in Madison, Illinois, in 1998.

But the finishing position did not matter as much as the opportunity; the feeling that Adam was in the right place. People inside and outside the garage acknowledged that. And in the weeks to come, his smile and outgoing style attracted so many fans. He proudly posed for photographs with his great-grandfather, Lee, grandfather, Richard, and dad, Kyle. It was a high-speed completely successful passing of the Petty baton. Or, at least it seemed to be.

Heartbreakingly, two years later, nineteen-year-old Adam was killed in a practice session crash May 12, 2000, at New Hampshire Motor Speedway, where he was attempting to make his second NASCAR Cup Series race. Obviously, the loss of Adam fundamentally changed his grieving father and granddad going forward, but both have remained an ingrained part of the sport as they so believe Adam would have wanted.

"When you look at the Pettys, from Lee to Richard to Kyle to Adam, you see the evolution of, perhaps, their greatest contribution to NASCAR—fan friendliness," said Eddie Gossage, a former track president who spent the bulk of his career in NASCAR.

"While Lee helped establish the sport during its rough-and-tumble formative years, Richard ushered the sport into a more modern age and two hundred visits to Victory Lane. But when the all-time king of the sport flashed his bright smile and stayed late to sign every autograph fans wanted, he set the tone for everybody else in the sport to follow his lead. Forever."

Through the glory, the challenges, the historic significance, and the personal heartbreak, the Pettys have been the steady force of competition and leadership in NASCAR. They are beloved to this day in a way like no other, mavericks in varying definitions, central pillars of a sport they helped craft and create.

Richard Petty got his two-hundredth and final NASCAR Cup Series victory at the 1984 Firecracker 400, and then celebrated with his favorite Republican—President Ronald Reagan.

1959 DAYTONA 500

THAT FEBRUARY AFTERNOON IN 1959 represented so much more than the formal debut of what would become NASCAR's preeminent race, now almost seventy years later still a celebration of speed, talent, and ingenuity that keeps the whole industry moving at breakneck speed.

The race, which wouldn't be officially named the Daytona 500 until 1961, was the first major event on the newly constructed 2.5-mile Daytona International Speedway—a model of technology and dream. The fifty-nine-car field for the epically named First 500-Mile NASCAR International Sweepstakes at Daytona, amazingly included two classes of race cars, including a twenty-count Convertible Division—a brand of cars that certainly seem almost unfathomable on the Daytona high banks today.

Living up to its high-stakes attention, the race ending was dramatic and controversial, everything the new stock car series could hope for in its Daytona superspeedway debut. Lee Petty, patriarch of the great NASCAR Petty family, and Johnny Beauchamp settled the caution-free race between them dueling it out in the final thirty laps.

With three laps to go they were door-to-door and took the Daytona checkered flag side-by-side. Each driver, Petty and Beauchamp, was absolutely convinced he had won the race, with Beauchamp even pulling into Victory Lane after the checkered flag, where he was declared the "unofficial winner." Petty, however, maintained, "I had Beauchamp by a good two feet [61 cm]. In my mind, I know I won." Even competitors such as Fireball Roberts—who was standing at the finish line after his car had been eliminated earlier in the day—immediately insisted Petty had unquestionably won the race.

Without the benefit of today's technology, it took three full days of seek-and-review before NASCAR President Bill France Sr. would declare a winner. France—who was actually on the flag stand for the finish—used photographs from the photographers covering the race and even newsreel footage to review the checkered flag moment. And he, ultimately, declared Petty as the race winner on the Wednesday after the race.

"The newsreel substantiated that the cars of Petty and Beauchamp did not change positions from the time those other still photographs were taken just before the finish," France explained. "Petty is the winner."

Ironically, the initial confusion about the race finish and the time it took for a proper review of NASCAR's huge event, played into France's hands and NASCAR's intrigue. The first version of today's Daytona 500 was thrilling on track and the controversial finish created further interest, extending the attention span.

The 1959 Daytona 500 delivered a new form of racing. The debut was so smooth there were zero cautions even on this new and daunting brand of mega venue. The two-hundred-lap race had six different leaders and delivered the kind of competition that NASCAR was all too ready to share with those eager to give this relatively "new" sport a try.

(OPPOSITE) **The first Daytona 500, February 22, 1959, was won by Lee Petty (No. 452) in a photo finish with Johnny Beauchamp (No. 73). The decision took several days to make. Pay no attention to the No. 48 running on the outside. It was a lap down.**

Firestone
MISS
500

CHAPTER 3

THE 1960s

DAYTONA DRIVES GROWTH IN ALL DIRECTIONS

The opening of Daytona International Speedway in 1959 began the next chapter of NASCAR racing. When the 1960s rolled around, things took off.

WITHIN THE NEXT FEW YEARS, larger speedways of a mile or more were built in Atlanta, Georgia, and Charlotte and Rockingham, North Carolina. The new tracks offered high speeds and wild action. The "Superspeedway Era" had been born. Television took notice, with all three of the major networks finding space in their schedules to broadcast major racing events.

The greater speeds required heavy-duty equipment, and aftermarket companies popped up offering specialized brakes, suspension parts, and engine components. Roll cage design was expanded to add rigidity to the car's frame and increased safety for the driver. Tire technology was increased to include a tire within a tire in case of a blowout on the big tracks. And fuel cells were included in each car to minimize the chance of fire.

Fidel Castro and his ragtag crew took over Cuba and the United States was in the midst of the Kennedy administration, or "Camelot." For a while, at least. Speaking of politics, George Wallace, the governor of Alabama, added his support to the building of the largest track to date, the Alabama International Motor Speedway, (today known as Talladega Superspeedway). It was the fastest track on the circuit and ushered in a new era of horsepower, aerodynamics, and drivers' intestinal fortitude.

Just over the horizon would be a deal to revolutionize the sport and open the door for major national sponsors. NASCAR had never seen anything like it.

JUNIOR JOHNSON

FOR THOSE WHO revere NASCAR's origins that made it an outlaw sport, we present an actual outlaw, right here, for your reading enjoyment, Robert Glenn Johnson Jr.

Junior will do just fine.

We're talking the original Junior, the *only* Junior for many old-school NASCAR fans. The Junior who hauled moonshine as a kid, then got busted—not on the road but at the still—as he was simply trying to light it up as his daddy had asked him to, when federal agents came flying out of the woods and took him away in 1956. Junior did eleven months in jail, costing him a season and a half of competition, both on the racetrack and on the moonshining backroads. (He was pardoned in 1986 by then-President Ronald Reagan.)

He didn't return to either jail or runnin' shine. Instead, he returned to racing, emboldened as always by the success of outrunning revenuers. Junior had won five races in 1955, his first full NASCAR Cup Series season. After his hiatus, things got serious. He won forty-five more times from 1958 to '66. He then quit driving to become a car owner. Things got even more serious. He won 132 races as an owner, fielding cars for two three-time Cup Series champions, Cale Yarborough and Darrell Waltrip.

Those statistics make him the only person in NASCAR history to achieve that level of two-tiered success, and they're the main reasons Junior was in the NASCAR Hall of Fame's inaugural inductee class in 2010. But not the only ones.

Start with that drafting thing. At the second Daytona 500 in 1960, drivers were trying to get around Daytona International Speedway as fast as possible. Tough puzzle, the 2.5-mile monstrosity with 31-degree banked turns. During practice that year, Junior figured out that if he rode tight behind a leading car's rear bumper, his car would go faster—while using less fuel. It was a "slipstream" effect that Johnson maximized. His car was not the fastest in the field. But it was first when the checkered flag flew, with drafting expertise the key. There really had been no invention, just discovery, Johnson pointed out for years afterward. He was just a good ol' boy, and sharp as a tack.

Junior never lost his Daytona touch as either a driver or owner. He qualified on the front row for the last Daytona 500 he ran, in 1965. Eight times his cars were on the pole. Six times his rides went to Victory Lane, the final time in '94 when Jimmy Spencer won the Pepsi 400.

"By [racing] on his own unmistakable terms, he became the unofficial king of this 'wild new thing' [called NASCAR] in the late 1950s and early 1960s," journalist Jonathan Ingram writes.

Junior was something. Junior was a legend—and an accessible one. Rare the instance when he wouldn't pick up the landline himself, at his home in North Wilkesboro, North Carolina, to speak to a NASCAR type, a media member, a fan—anyone.

Had something to do with authenticity. Remember that?

"People called him 'country smart,'" said journalist Mike Hembree, who has written more on Junior than just about anyone, which seems like a helluva fun time.

Victory Lane at Daytona International Speedway was considerably more casual in 1960 than what you see today. At least it sure looks that way with ol' Junior and his car owner, Ray Fox, celebrating with the boys, atop his race car. The old moonshiner is enjoying a Pepsi, which makes this photo sublime *and* surreal.

Junior Johnson and Curtis Turner duel on the high banks during the 1960 Daytona 500, won by Johnson. This photo looks like a slingshot/inside pass move, after Johnson had utilized the draft to suck up behind Turner's car before zipping down low and past. At least that's what might've happened here—and probably did.

"And he was comfortable in every situation, from the Detroit boardroom to the convenience store down the street from his garage. You know, he was just that kind of guy.

"And you could not outflank him. You knew that he always held an ace somewhere or other, even if it was something he didn't necessarily know a lot about. He could use his country wiles or whatever you want to call it . . . you just weren't going to get anything over on him."

The NASCAR Hall of Fame called Junior "one of the sport's most enduring—and endearing—personalities in NASCAR" when he was inducted in 2010. Legendary journalist Tom Wolfe had that figured out in 1965 and assembled the seminal piece "The Last American Hero Is Junior Johnson. Yes!" for *Esquire* magazine.

"Junior Johnson," Wolfe wrote, "is one of the last of those sports stars who is not just an ace at the game itself, but a hero a whole people or class of people can identify with."

Accordingly, people continued to identify with Junior long after his racing days were through, right up until his 2019 death. It should be noted that the moonshine helped. Legal, this time around. In his later years, Junior got a moonshine deal with a company called Midnight Moon. He gave the company his recipe. Whereupon everyone started printing money.

Yes!

WENDELL SCOTT

WENDELL SCOTT was one of the automatic subjects for these pages, the latest in a rush of acknowledgments that have come Scott's way over the last two decades, the pinnacle being his 2015 induction into the NASCAR Hall of Fame. Well deserved, and it shone a long-overdue spotlight on the late Scott, the first African American to win a NASCAR Cup Series race.

Admiration for Scott hinges on far more than that sole victory in 495 Cup Series starts from 1961 to '73. People who were there remember Scott more for his underfunded efforts than his accomplishments.

But let's not miss the point here: The efforts *were* the accomplishments.

To say he persevered would be an understatement of the first degree, racing all those years with Confederate flags flying in the infields amid a sea of discrimination few could have imagined. The N-word was the preferred term for Black people in many places where NASCAR raced. Death threats were a regular occurrence.

It's important to know, however, that Scott still had friends in the business and the garage area. Good thing.

Scott became an expert improvisational mechanic during World War II, spending his three years in the army working in a motor pool. Side bet: The jeeps were in better shape than many of the stock cars he would climb into in coming years. The photographs of Scott's NASCAR years are classic, and many showed him and his sons working together under the same hood of some beat-up machine, Wendell especially covered in oil and grime.

Scott may not have had much, but he had family. Wife Mary, sons Wendell Jr. and Frank, daughters Ann, Deborah, Kay, and Sybil—all were regulars at the racetracks. Junior and Frankie formed the pit crew. If the car needed real work, the driver hoped and became the crew chief. Mary home-cooked up a storm and fed half the garage, the stories go.

And he had that one victory at Speedway Park in Jacksonville, Florida, in 1963, his badge of statistical honor, along with twenty top-five finishes and 147 top tens. He finished in the top fifteen of the NASCAR Cup Series final standings eight consecutive seasons, from 1963 to '70, with his best points finish sixth in 1966.

That victory was scarred. NASCAR didn't award the winner's trophy to Scott, perhaps fearing a negative crowd reaction, since Jacksonville wasn't exactly welcoming. Scott died in 1990; his family got a custom-crafted replacement trophy from NASCAR in 2021.

"There were a lot of detractors [during his career]," said Scott's son Frank at the Hall of Fame induction ceremony. "But humility and integrity were stamped all over his interactions across the country dealing with people that didn't necessarily like him.

Wendell Scott started his racing career in modifieds he built from scratch, like the beauty shown here. Nobody ever did more with less in NASCAR.

(RIGHT) **Wendell Scott's main pit crew members were always his sons Frankie (*left*) and Wendell Jr. (*center*). Here, the Scotts are tinkering with an engine in their backyard, in Danville, Virginia.**

(OPPOSITE) **Wendell Scott never had it easy in his NASCAR career. This shot could serve as a microcosm of that career: Scott perusing his wrecked ride at Asheville-Weaverville Speedway in November 1967.**

"He didn't hold grudges. He would forgive you if you mistreated him [on the racetrack]. . . . He broke the glass ceiling."

By any reasonable estimation, Scott could've been a championship contender, with first-rate cars, sponsorship support, and more dudes to help his sons handle pit stops. More than one old-timer has been quoted as saying Scott was one of the most talented drivers around in the sixties, which makes this, ultimately, a bittersweet yarn.

Brian Donovan, in his Scott biography, *Hard Driving*, maintains that Scott's career troubled him throughout his post-racing life. "The fact that all of his courage and effort did not ultimately produce an unarguable answer to the fundamental question in every racer's career—Was he really a driver of the first rank?—remained for Scott a painful hole in his life," Donovan writes.

Bittersweet, but the great Wendell Scott deserves whatever mentions come his way, and he always will. If you don't love this guy, this guy's legacy, then shame on you. So, consider this another mention. And here's to many more.

(continues on page 74)

34
WYNN'S
PREMIER
PURE

MAMIE REYNOLDS

MAMIE REYNOLDS DID SO MUCH during her life, so why not NASCAR? The woman was a multitasking maverick. One with money, it should be noted. Which helped when it came to fielding cars in the NASCAR Cup Series in the early 1960s.

Cup was called Grand National back then and grand it was to have Reynolds involved, her two years of car ownership followed by other ventures similarly ambitious.

Reynolds took that life-well-lived stuff to the max. Why not? She was heir to a mining fortune. Her family once owned the Hope Diamond, which must have been worth something.

Her father, Democratic senator Robert Rice Reynolds, maxed out somewhat too. Five marriages. Tons of political drama. Mamie's mother, Evalyn Washington McLean—the fifth wife—died when she was twenty-four, due to an accidental drug overdose.

(OPPOSITE) **Mamie Reynolds was an heiress in the R. J. Reynolds family—and a nineteen-year-old car owner in the NASCAR Cup Series in 1962 to '63. She's shown here with Darel Dieringer, who drove five races for her in the '62 season.**

Some have likened Reynolds' life story to sounding more like fiction than fact. Upon further review, *that's* a fact. An abridged Reynolds rundown—and it's all true:

- Short track racer, drag racer.
- 1962: NASCAR car owner at the age of nineteen.
- 1962: First female car owner to win in the Cup Series, with NASCAR Hall of Famer Fred Lorenzen as driver.
- 1963: First female owner to field a car in the Daytona 500.
- 1963: Winning car owner in the Daytona Continental.
- 1963: Married Luigi Coco Chinetti Jr., son of the three-time 24 Hours of Le Mans winner. They were both twenty. Lasted two years. The day they divorced, damned if Mamie didn't get married again, this time for good, to Joe Gregory.
- First owner of the American Basketball Association's Kentucky Colonels. Remember those cats? Louie Dampier, Artis Gilmore, Dan Issel. Different kind of super team.
- Big-time American Kennel Club champion dog owner. That's how she met Gregory.
- Bigger-time socialite in Asheville, North Carolina, where she lived for years, hosting parties that became legendary.

The NASCAR victory came on September 13, 1962, at Augusta (Georgia) Speedway, Lorenzen leading nineteen of two hundred laps. Atlanta Motor Speedway. The next season, Ed Livingston put her car into the Daytona 500 field; later in the year, Darel Dieringer had a top five. After that, Reynolds moved on, leading a remarkable life.

She died in 2014 at the age of seventy-two.

385 HP
26
Dieringer
26
MICRO-PRECISION
Firestone
FORD

Mario Andretti en route to being one of the greatest drivers in the history of IndyCar racing, took a quick break in 1967 to pull off an upset victory in the Daytona 500.

MARIO ANDRETTI

THERE WAS PERHAPS no better litmus test of NASCAR's early popularity than the fact that some of the most highly regarded, internationally accomplished drivers so wanted to participate in American stock car racing's most important event, the Daytona 500.

For the legend Mario Andretti, he not only competed in the race, but he also won the 1967 Daytona 500 and, to that point, it was his time on the Daytona high banks in that No. 11 red-white-and-blue Ford that represented the high mark of an absolutely epic career.

We tend to think of Andretti for all his open wheel accomplishments—from the 1967 Indianapolis 500 Rookie of the Year honor to his 1969 Indianapolis 500 win, from his four IndyCar championships to the 1978 Formula 1 title. He also won the Twelve Hours of Sebring overall, twice. He earned a watch winning overall in the Rolex 24 at Daytona. And he proved himself versatile enough to also win the famed Pikes Peak International Hill Climb.

But it was that Florida February afternoon in 1969, going door to door, fender to fender with NASCAR's best, that loudly punctuates the beginning of Andretti's incredible résumé and shows the uncommon versatility that makes Andretti both a maverick and a legend.

That 1967 Daytona 500 was actually the seventh NASCAR race Andretti had competed in. He made his debut on the famed Riverside, California, road course in 1966 with a sixteenth-place finish among forty-four cars. But four of his next five NASCAR starts came at Daytona, including qualifying races.

A crash only thirty-one laps into his 1966 Daytona 500 debut relegated Andretti to a thirty-seventh-place finish driving for no other than the legendary Smokey Yunick. The fact that these two greats—Andretti and Yunick—paired only adds to the folklore of Mario and the Daytona 500. Andretti would earn a thirty-first-place showing in the summer 1966 Daytona race for Yunick. And considering what was to come, it was noteworthy that Andretti didn't have a top ten in his first five starts at the big track.

But Andretti would return to Daytona in 1967 to leave his historical mark. A sixth-place finish in the No. 11 Holman-Moody Racing Ford in the Daytona 500 qualifying race certainly raised hopes.

Andretti's encouraging finish in that qualifier put him up front early in the Daytona 500. But it was NASCAR stalwarts Curtis Turner and LeeRoy Yarbrough starting on the front row and leading the first laps.

Only twenty-three laps into the race, Andretti negotiated the lead away and he would go on to turn in a dominant drive that fully withstands modern era judgment—leading 112 of the 200 laps—outmaneuvering, outracing, and just plain outdoing even his own expectations.

On the day, Andretti led nine different times, but it was an amazing give-and-take at the end of the race that cemented his impact on the field and the form. His door-to-door racing against NASCAR Hall of Famers David Pearson and Andretti's Daytona teammate Fred Lorenzen absolutely thrilled the speedway crowd and would go on to become the storylines of Daytona 500 legend.

Mario Andretti used a unique approach to navigating the 2.5-mile Daytona International Speedway track in 1967—and winning the Daytona 500. Using his experience gleaned at other high banks, Andretti drove his Ford Fairlane up against the retaining wall for much of the race, sliding and smoking right rear tires. In the process, he smoked the field.

Early in the race, his car's low rear spoiler created a unique situation that caused many drivers not to run too close to him. He qualified and practiced with that race-ready spoiler that essentially made his competitors uncomfortable in tight quarters. So, in the race, the safest most efficient place for Andretti was out front.

"I learned to deal with it," Andretti recalled in a recent IndyCar.com article. "For 500 miles, I never turned left. I went into the corner neutral with the steering to the right."

There was a certain amount of trust Andretti earned in the way he raced that day. And he has always insisted the stock car drivers welcomed him and appreciated his game. Certainly, after his dominant effort that Sunday afternoon in NASCAR's highest profile race, Andretti could count himself a viable stock car driver.

"Arguably, the Daytona 500 win at that time was the biggest event of my career and particularly satisfying to do it somewhere where it wasn't my specialty," Andretti would later tell IndyCar reporters. "Can you imagine the same thing if one of their drivers—Richard Petty or David Pearson—had come to Indy and won the Indy 500?

"It had a special sound to it and it still does, actually."

This pressure to succeed in another genre was really more self-involved. Expectations were there, of course, but more muted as Andretti tried to become the first big-name open wheel devotee to truly go after the greatest stock car trophy in the world.

And he did it. He earned it. He celebrated it.

"I always felt welcome, quite honestly," Andretti shared. "There were no issues there that I could feel or detect. It was a matter of earning my way through and trying to gain some respect. Obviously, I'm sure some of those drivers were laughing at us thinking we were in the wrong place. That is what created a great challenge for all of us from open wheel.

Henry Neil Castles was known as Soapy since he was a kid, racing in the Soap Box Derby. As an adult, he personified the underdog label on the race track. Off track, Soapy became one of the world's top car-driving stuntmen for filmmaking.

SOAPY CASTLES

IT'S A GOOD nickname that Henry Neil "Soapy" Castles carried throughout his eighty-seven years on our orb, but one that belied his determination and his accomplishments. Not really sure what the connotation is when it comes to a moniker like Soapy, but it seems/sounds soft.

Castles was anything but.

NASCAR legend Buddy Shuman came up with "Soapy" when Neil was only nine, after he gave the kid some wheels for a Soap Box Derby car. Shuman was Castles' window into NASCAR. Castles took a peek, liked what he saw, and as an adult would race from 1957 to 1976 in the NASCAR Cup Series.

After those twenty-one years, the stats weren't kind. Four hundred ninety-eight starts, zero victories. You can't be soft and endure that much failure.

Then, again, one man's failure can be the same man's paycheck. It's all relative and for Soapy it was all about having a job and raising a family. Even without winning a Cup Series race, Castles won nearly $300,000 in his career. Fifty-one top-five finishes helped. He was the champion of NASCAR's old Grand National East Series in 1972, winning twice that season. In '73 he finished second in the series standings.

Castles' other career brought him more notoriety. It started almost as a lark, in 1957 at the old Occoneechee Speedway in Hillsborough, North Carolina. Castles and some other boys were hired to drive in a racing scene for a movie. The designated stunt driver, who was scripted to crash a car, never showed. Castles volunteered, flipped the car first class the next day, and found a second calling. He became a serious Hollywood stunt man, flipping and crashing cars on purpose.

When his new line of work started flourishing, he figured he had made the right choice, since he had been upside down many times anyway in a car as a racer. And besides, the money was good. Castles, who died in 2022, used to tell people that if it wasn't for stunt driving, he wouldn't have been able to keep racing.

His biggest movie was 1968's *Speedway* starring Elvis Presley, with much of it shot at Charlotte Motor Speedway. Castles said he wrecked a bunch of cars for that film, as Elvis's double. Other notable movies he worked on included *Greased Lightning* starring Richard Pryor (1977) and *Six Pack* starring Kenny Rogers (1982). He even had a few small roles.

"Between NASCAR and the Screen Actors Guild, it's the best thing I've ever [done]," Castles said.

"To many race fans, Neil Castles was an independent in NASCAR's premier series, who seemed to always play second fiddle to those teams that either were factory backed or possessed a high-profile sponsor," wrote journalist and author Deb Williams in the foreword to Castles autobiography.

"However, the man who acquired the nickname Soapy during his Soap Box Derby days was so much more . . . It was Neil Castles' philosophy that led him to experience one of racing's most intriguing stories. He believed that something odd would happen every day. And as his [life] shows, it did."

Driving the No. 21 Ford of the famed Wood Brothers Racing team, IndyCar star A. J. Foyt won the Daytona 500 in 1972.

A. J. FOYT

IN SO MANY WAYS, the great Texas racer A. J. Foyt was always more maverick than anyone else ever lined up alongside him on the starting grid. He could drive any type of race car, beat any type of champion race driver, and do it all with a grin and a wink that only made his competitors respect his talent more.

At 6 foot 1 (1 m 83 cm), the Texas-tough rancher was built more like a football player than any delicate car jockey but he sure proved himself up for the task—no matter the car, the competition, the track, or the stakes.

Foyt started his iconic career racing sprint cars and midgets. He moved up the open wheel ranks to eventually claim a record four Indianapolis 500s and seven USAC Series championships. He won the Rolex 24 at Daytona twice and even the 1967 24 Hours of Le Mans, but it was his foray in the stock cars that certainly seemed to suit his brash style. He loved the challenge of door-to-door racing against the best. And he loved to beat 'em—something he did in historical stride.

Foyt had already won a pair of USAC national championships, the 1961 Indy 500, and become a household name among fans and racers alike before even taking a seat in one of NASCAR's stock cars.

His first NASCAR race was none too surprisingly at the Riverside, California, road course where so many of his fellow open wheelers loved to run. Foyt finished runner-up by thirty-six seconds to another racing icon, the late Dan Gurney, who dominated the day leading 120 of the 185 laps. The pair were the only two drivers on the lead lap with fourth-place Fireball Roberts representing the NASCAR regulars that January 1963 afternoon.

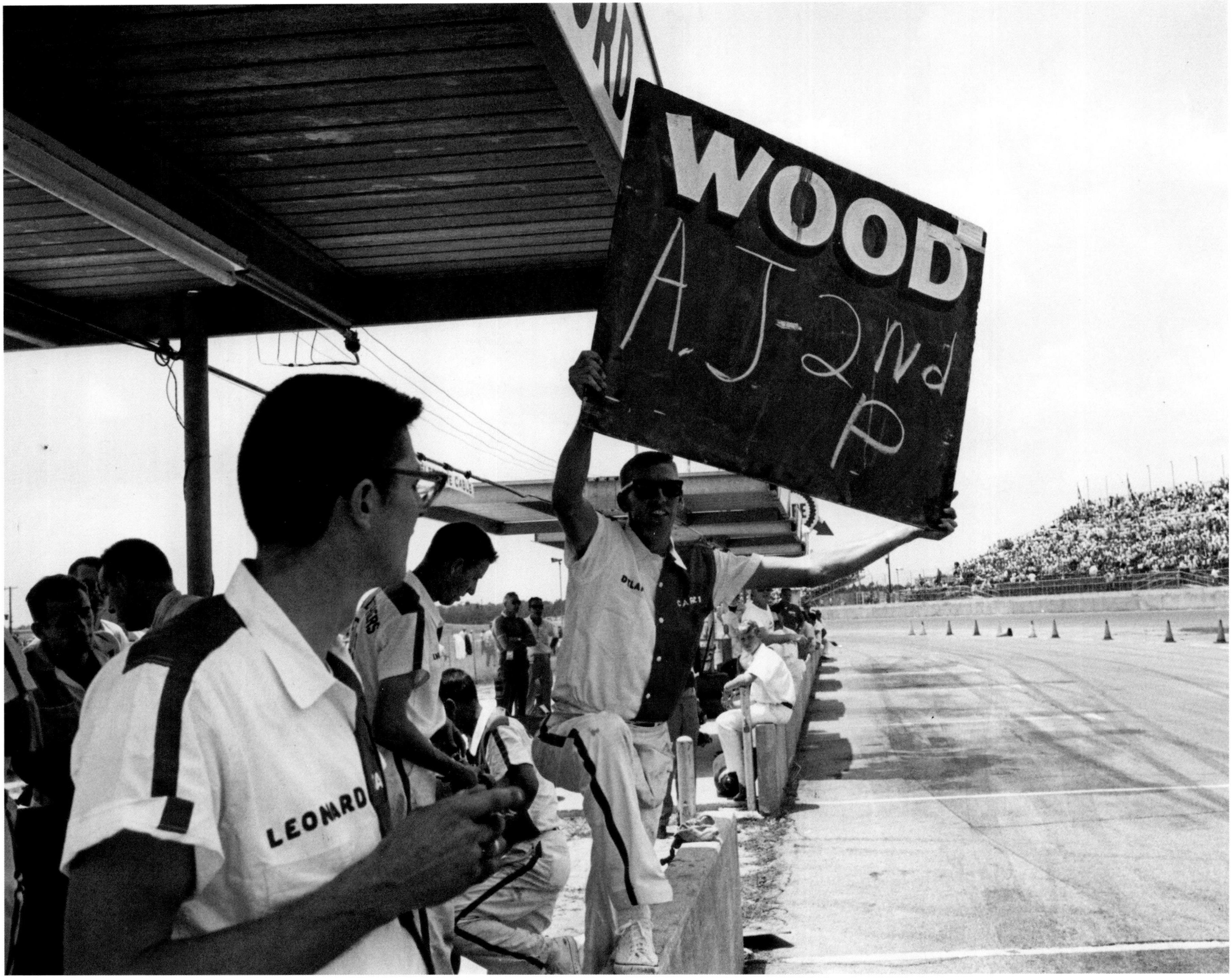
WOOD
A.J.-2nd
P
LEONARD

It was exactly the confidence boost Foyt may—or may not—have needed but he showed up for his next race, the Daytona 500, a month later ready to give the 2.5-mile Daytona International Speedway high banks his best. He finished third behind his teammate Paul Goldsmith in his first qualifying race, which was won by NASCAR Hall of Famer Junior Johnson.

Foyt led six laps and finished twenty-seventh in that 1963 Daytona 500 debut a few days later, completing 143 of the 200 laps. His final status was listed as "spin out." Perhaps fittingly, Foyt would finish a position behind another racing "maverick" that afternoon, African American driver Wendell Scott.

The Foyt NASCAR education was now full speed and "Super Tex," as he became known, was all in. It took a mere eleven races for him to hoist his first NASCAR trophy at Daytona's July Fourth 400 miler in 1964. And so the great open wheeler could certifiably count stock car racing among his gifts as well, a big hard-earned trophy to prove it.

He loved to go door to door with the stock car "boys" who appreciated his moxie and talent in equal servings.

In all, Foyt won seven NASCAR races in a diverse professional career that spanned thirty-nine years, from his 1957 USAC maiden start at Springfield, Illinois, to IndyCars to sports cars to stock cars to a pair of NASCAR Craftsman Truck Series races in 1996.

Chief among those victories was the 1972 Daytona 500 for the similarly legendary Wood Brothers Racing team. Foyt led an amazing 167 of the 200 laps to claim that historic Daytona win by a full lap over the field, giving him victories in America's two most esteemed events: the Daytona 500 and Indianapolis 500 (1961, '64, '67, and '77).

Open wheel or fenders on, Foyt was unstoppable when he was on top of his game.

Of that famous 1972 Daytona 500 win, Foyt still smiles decades later telling reporters on a Daytona visit in 2019, "I had everybody covered, it was a runaway. I knew I had it won when they dropped the green flag. I knew I had a fast car and would have great pit stops if I stayed out of trouble."

Foyt would go on to become the first driver to win four Indianapolis 500s and the first to hoist the Indy winner's Borg-Warner Trophy as a driver and a team owner, capturing the 1999 Indy 500 win with driver Kenny Brack.

None too surprisingly, even after retiring from the driver's seat, Foyt remained a passionate competitor—from famously tossing a laptop computer from a trackside scoring stand to physically confronting another driver in the Texas Motor Speedway Victory Lane after a disagreement over the race outcome.

And Foyt still smiles knowing that even though the scoring officials may have changed the finish of that 1997 race at Texas, he still has that original trophy in his Houston office.

Even closing in on his ninetieth birthday, Foyt is most happy at the racetrack and still making calls from pit road with his son Larry Foyt running the A. J. Foyt Racing team operations.

A. J. Foyt was one of the original mavericks, as tough outside the race car as he was talented in it. His talent and gumption may never be equaled, but they have always been appreciated.

"And I wouldn't change nothing," Foyt said.

(continues on page 82)

(OPPOSITE) **A big reason Foyt won the Daytona 500 is because he had the best pit crew in the business at that time, the Wood Brothers. Here, Delano Wood lets A. J. know he's in second place as he passes pit road.**

TIGER TOM PISTONE

IN 1960, the year of the second annual Daytona 500, drivers like "Tiger" Tom Pistone were in discovery mode.

Drafting, the new, nose-to-tail aerodynamic "tow" phenomenon, was manifesting on the outlandish 31-degree banked, 2.5-mile Daytona International Speedway tri-oval. Taming the high banks in traffic—the new game in town.

In the middle of the massive racetrack, another item was causing concern. Like the banking, it was something never before seen prior to DIS's 1959 opening. An actual lake, right in the middle of the expansive facility. Stocked with bass and everything, courtesy of the state of Florida and Bill France Sr. Lake Lloyd, named after France's buddy and longtime car dealer, Saxton Lloyd.

At some point during those first two years, more than one driver decided to pack a life vest into his stock car. Seriously. There are no definitive stats on life vests but it's reasonably certain that drivers collectively freaked out when Tommy Irwin's Ford Thunderbird went body surfing on the first lap of the first qualifying race for the 1960 Daytona 500. Irwin's car came flying off the backstretch, spinning, eventually going waterfront. Irwin hopped out before the car sank into the lakebed. The Ford sat there, partially submerged, for two days before being towed out, and into NASCAR lore.

"Tiger" Tom Pistone, a character *with* character. A part-time prankster but first and foremost, an outstanding racer. He had four victories at the NASCAR national series level, two apiece in the Cup Series and Convertible Division. Versatile fellow, Tiger. As of 2024, the race car/race parts business he started in the 1960s was still doing business. Pistone was also a renowned car builder.

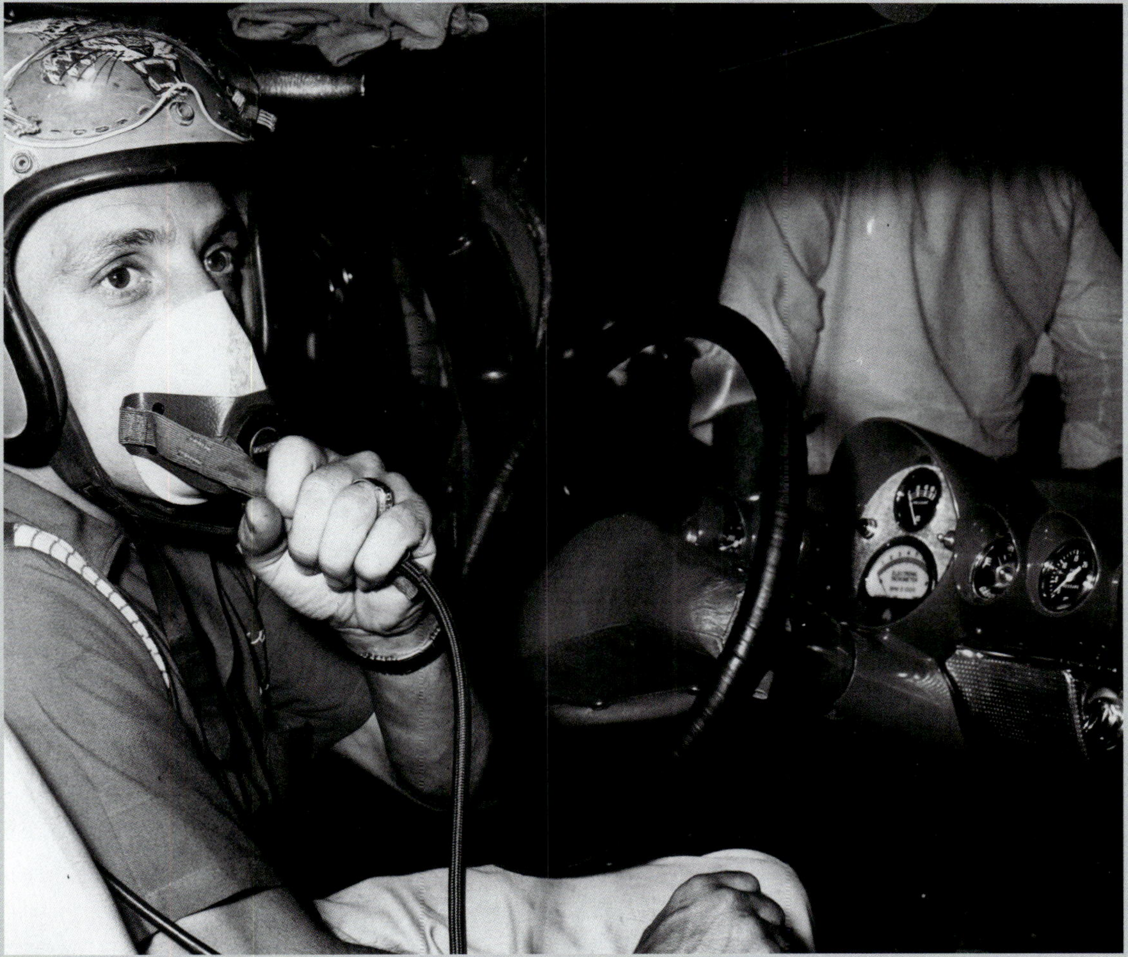

Daytona's 2.5-mile length and 31-degree banking were unsettling enough. Lake Lloyd, looming in the middle of it all, freaked out drivers further. Tiger Tom Pistone was a big pussycat, installing an oxygen tank and mask in his car in 1960. Give the Tig a break. He had watched another driver plunge his car into the water. Pistone couldn't swim.

When Irwin went into the drink, Tiger Tom Pistone had seen enough. He started the Daytona 500 with a life vest, oxygen tank, and face mask. Just in case.

"I couldn't swim and I wanted to make sure I'd be okay," Pistone said.

NASCAR Chairman and CEO Jim France, interviewed for this book, made a point to emphasize Pistone's maverick-style contributions, saying, "Tiger Tom, you need to include him. He was a real character, always. But he was first a racer—and a good one. And he was liked by darn near everyone."

Of course, the oxygen tank tale has blown everything else out of the water (bad pun, we know) when it comes to Pistone. The Chicago-area native—the good ol' boys called him "The Converted Yankee"—could drive the hell out of a short track. Some old-timers still around call Pistone the greatest short track racer ever. Fans of Ralph Earnhardt, Jack Ingram, or Dick Trickle would argue that, but no doubt Tiger Tom is in the discussion.

As for Daytona International Speedway, including Lake Lloyd, "It was just gorgeous. And I took to that track really fast. Curtis Turner and I learned about the draft and we were two of the fastest cars down there."

Pistone won two NASCAR Cup Series races, along with two NASCAR Convertible Division races in his career. But he also won Soldier Field track championships five times in the 1950s.

Before ending our talk, the oxygen mask had to be revisited. Could it have really helped, if he'd been submerged?

"Oh, yeah, it worked good."

Here they are, NASCAR's beloved Wood Brothers racing from their days of CITGO sponsorship: from left, Eddie, Len, their father, Glen, and uncle, Leonard.

THE WOOD BROTHERS

THE WOOD BROTHERS are on the cover of this book, as they damn well should be, and not only because of the quality of the iconic pit stop photo chosen. There were thousands of such stops through the years because the Woods were revolutionizing the art of pitting and, in the process, changing not only NASCAR but auto racing overall.

Oil-stained choreography came to NASCAR's pit road in the 1960s when the Wood Brothers started figuring out how to perform such an important task as a team, and setting a standard that would be hard to match. Pit stops had never really been emphasized as vital. Occasionally, they bordered on the leisurely. It was a case of "get 'er dun" instead of "do it well."

Leonard Wood, co-founder with his late brother Glen, of the Wood Brothers organization, said his team started working on refining pit stops in 1961. A Ford Motor Company man watched NASCAR's pit road action long enough—probably didn't take that long—to tell Leonard, "I think there's time to be gained in the pits."

"And, of course, we wanted to impress Ford Motor Company, so we started working on it right then," Wood said.

Leonard Wood served for years as the team's crew chief. Ever an inventor, Wood devised a jack that required fewer pumps to elevate the car. He had modified fuel cans to make the gas empty into the tank faster. You ought to see the lawn tractor he built from scratch. Another story.

Leonard and Glen recruited their brothers Clay, Delano, and Ray to become crewmen. As the organization grew, Leonard stuck with the racing operation while Glen concentrated on the business side.

Leonard remembers that rivals didn't really pay much attention to their pit road synchronicity. At first.

"They took it serious after we started winning," an eighty-eight-year-old Wood said in 2024. "We'd come out of a pit stop and be a half lap ahead. It didn't take them long. They saw the light."

Which meant garagewide catch-up. The brothers were altering the NASCAR landscape, one pit stop at a time.

They started by timing the top combo of driver Fireball Roberts and crew chief Smokey Yunick. First clocking: forty-five seconds for two tires and gas. "So right away we started working on that," Leonard said, "and soon we're down to twenty seconds. We kept working on it."

People noticed. For the 1965 Indianapolis 500, Ford brought the Woods to the Brickyard to crew Lotus-Fords driven by international star Jim Clark and Bobby Johns. They did, and Clark won. Two pit stops for the whole race, fuel only, solid twenty-four seconds each. Johns, finishing eighth, also pitted twice.

The trip to Indy should never be minimized when it comes to the brothers' legacy. Outsiders to say the least, they helped Clark win by nearly *two minutes*.

"I'm thinking, 'Here we are going in . . . how are they going to accept us?'" Leonard Wood told journalist Bruce Martin in 2000. "After they welcomed us being there, it worked fine. Then we took over the pit stops. They gave us a free hand to do what we needed to do on that end of it.

"We had already won the Daytona 500, so what you do then is get your mind set on preparing the car for a pit stop. Indianapolis was a big event, with three hundred thousand people and [everyone] crowded around you, but we concentrated on doing our thing."

The Wood Brothers were heroes back home in Virginia and throughout the Southeast. They had showed those Yankees up there. The little Scottish guy, he was pretty good too. And how about that headline in the Columbia (South Carolina) state newspaper, the morning after Indy? "General Lee Would've Been Proud of Native Sons."

Having won America's two biggest auto races in a two-year span, the Wood Brothers were stars too and would stay that way. So were their drivers: David Pearson, A. J. Foyt, Donnie Allison, Cale Yarborough, and Neil Bonnett, in Mercury Cyclones and Montegos. Pearson was the definitive Wood Brothers driver until a late-career (1979) rift; he won forty-three races himself in the seventies.

Wood Brothers Racing, based as always in Stuart, Virginia, continues to field a team in the NASCAR Cup Series, with Fords driven by Harrison Burton, son of former top NASCAR driver Jeff Burton. Glen Wood's sons, Eddie and Len, now head the team. In 2017, they won the Daytona 500 for the fifth time, with driver Trevor Bayne—forty-one years after the fourth triumph with David Pearson.

Glen died in 2019. He was inducted into the NASCAR Hall of Fame in 2012. Leonard followed his brother into the NASCAR Hall of Fame in 2013.

(ABOVE LEFT) **This 1978 photo from Charlotte Motor Speedway is our *NASCAR Mavericks* cover shot, because it has it all—the crowd, the choreography, and the air hose expertise of crew chief Leonard Wood, who used both hands and feet to maneuver that piece of equipment.**

(ABOVE RIGHT) **Yes, that's Glen Wood hauling tires through the NASCAR garage. Glen Wood, one of NASCAR's 50 Greatest Drivers, Glen Wood, NASCAR Hall of Fame inductee. In those days, he did whatever it took. Glen's early racing success established the Wood Brothers in NASCAR.**

RACEWAY
71
22

CHAPTER 4

THE 1970s

CORPORATE AMERICA, NETWORK TV COMES TO NASCAR

This decade saw the biggest changes in the sport. With major sponsorship behind the series, each race became a grand event. Gone were the 100 milers on ½-mile tracks. Now, each race would be at least 250 miles and held on major speedways. And to put the icing on the cake, many races would be televised, which made it much easier for teams to gain a full-time sponsor.

THE BIGGER PURSES and TV exposure drew many new drivers including females, foreign drivers, and even a country western singing star. The Ford and Chrysler factories were on their toes creating radical, aerodynamic machines, and the competition between them became known as the "Aero Wars," adding new interest to the sport for the fans.

The Vietnam War finally ended, allowing many young gearheads to come home and pursue their racing interests. They were looking for the rush they experienced during battle and many of them became fearless short track drivers who "took no prisoners" on the track in hopes of working their way up to racing's top tier.

The sport got a major shot in the arm with the first flag-to-flag television broadcast of the Daytona 500 by CBS. The lead came down to two drivers, Cale Yarborough and Donnie Allison, battling for the win on the last lap. They bumped and then crashed causing the third-place driver, Richard Petty, to win in a near photo finish. A major snowstorm had blanketed the East Coast, leaving much of America with nothing to do but watch TV and the only show of substance was the 500 broadcast. The two drivers and Allison's brother, Bobby, got into a melee after the race, causing NASCAR racing to enjoy a new nationwide interest and expand its fan base by millions.

(PREVIOUS) **Winged Warriors: Bobby Allison (22) and Bobby Isaac (71)—both driving Dodge Daytonas—and Richard Petty's (43) Plymouth Superbird battle on the Riverside road course in 1970.**

Smoke 'em if you got 'em. And back then, it seemed like everyone did. After R. J. Reynolds started sponsoring NASCAR's Grand National Division—it became known as the NASCAR Winston Cup Series—signage was everywhere, at every racetrack.

THE REVOLUTIONARY R. J. REYNOLDS SPONSORSHIP

THE STORY IS TRUE, and Robert Glenn "Junior" Johnson always seemed to have it just about memorized whenever he was asked to recount how he, somewhat accidentally, brokered the deal that led R. J. Reynolds Tobacco to sponsor what would become the NASCAR Winston Cup Series.

Before the 1971 season, driver-turned-owner Johnson needed support for his own race team. He secured a meeting with R. J. Reynolds representatives, but before the meeting was knee deep, RJR shifted focus to a much larger picture, with all due respect to Junior. They weren't blowing smoke.

Give Johnson big-time credit. He knew the landscape going in and thought he could score, just like the old days. In and out, grab the cash and haul ass. See, the government had banned tobacco advertising from television and Junior Johnson figured they might have some extra coin on a spreadsheet somewhere. Junior wasn't a spreadsheet guy, but you get the idea.

"I told them I wanted eight hundred and fifty thousand dollars to run my car for a year," Johnson recalled in 2002. "They just sorta laughed at me. So, I asked them if that was too much. That's when they told me no, that they were looking for something a lot bigger. They said that with them having to come off of TV, they had five hundred and seventy-five million dollars that they had to do something with. I said, 'Lord, have mercy, you need to go to Bill France Sr. about sponsoring NASCAR's whole deal.'"

Lord, have mercy, they did, making what Johnson called a match made in heaven. Not sure about the heavenly part but the deal did seem to make sense, beyond the large amount of money on the table. NASCAR, a sport that started with moonshiners, would now be sponsored by tobacco.

(RIGHT) **The inimitable Ralph Seagraves, an RJR executive and promotional leader dressed like a walking pack of Winstons, helped define the new era of corporate sponsorship coming to NASCAR.**

(FAR RIGHT) **Jerry Long, CEO of the R. J. Reynolds Tobacco Company, speaks at a season-ending NASCAR banquet at the Waldorf Astoria in New York.**

Back to the money. In 1971, the headlining NASCAR Grand National Division had select races (of at least 250 miles designated as "Winston Cup races" with a $100,000 point fund paid out at the end of the year. In 1972, the sponsorship covered the entire season for the newly named NASCAR Winston Cup Grand National Division. Big change. But not the only one. NASCAR cut the schedule from forty-eight to thirty-one races. Henceforth, NASCAR statisticians would be charting the "Modern Era."

In 1986, the NASCAR Winston Cup Series became the new title, one of professional sports' most iconic brands, and lasted through the 2003 season, when NASCAR and R. J. Reynolds ended their relationship after thirty-three seasons.

The sponsorship was absolutely essential to NASCAR's growth, and not only at the top level. Winston sponsored NASCAR's weekly racing series for twenty years. There were also special events that paid big bucks for the Cup Series. NASCAR's all-star race was known as The Winston, paying a million to the champion. The Winston Million program paid another million to a driver winning three of the four (or sweeping) designated major events: Daytona 500, Winston 500 (you know it), Coca-Cola 600, and Southern 500.

In the early years of the deal, with Winston running flat-out to market the sport, a now-legendary 100 percent maverick was front and center at the races, making friends and promoting product. Ralph Seagraves wore some outlandish outfits, making him look like a walking pack of Winstons. Which was fine with Ralph, who led RJR's Special Events Operations department, which came to be called Sports Marketing Enterprises, from 1972 to '85. Ralph was at that first RJR meeting with Junior. He was going to make sure this deal worked.

It did. The sponsorship set the standard for sports marketing in so many ways, the sponsor's controversial product notwithstanding.

Times were different.

THE PLYMOUTH SUPERBIRD

THE PLYMOUTH SUPERBIRD must be the most significant one-and-done deal in NASCAR history. The year was 1970 and the cars were exotic—and fast. And destined to be obsoleted from competition via the NASCAR rulebook.

Superbirds were inspired by the Dodge Charger Daytonas, along with the need to lure Richard Petty back to the Plymouth fold. Petty, a longtime Plymouth standard-bearer, had wanted a more exotic car, preferably with a wing attached, to race in NASCAR's top series. Plymouth didn't have one ready, so Petty jumped to Ford for the '69 season and drove fast-back-style Torinos.

Dodge Daytonas rolled out that year, featuring a 23-inch (58 cm) rear wing and wedge-shaped nose. They were different. They looked fast. They debuted at brand-new Talladega Superspeedway in September. That was the race where drivers protested, boycotting due to safety concerns, at the 2.66-mile monster tri-oval. Bill France Sr. assembled a make-do field of second-tier drivers. Richard Brickhouse drove a Daytona to the win.

In 1970, Petty came back home to drive the new Superbirds, modified Roadrunners remembered mainly for those exotic wings and sleek bodies that made "Petty Blue" look better than ever. There was more to the machines than aerodynamics, like a big-block 426 Hemi V8 engine producing 425 horsepower. Zero to 60 in 5½ seconds. Gary Romberg, a NASA engineer who helped design the Saturn 1B booster that carried astronauts to the moon, was hired by Chrysler to work on the Superbird project.

"Richard's heart was really with Chrysler," said NASCAR historian Buz McKim, "and when he had a chance to go back with Chrysler, he just jumped at it. And those Superbirds, man, as cool as the Chargers were, the Superbirds were even cooler. They just had a special look. A little leaner and just a beautiful, beautiful race car."

Superbirds and Daytonas combined to win thirty-three of the season's forty-eight races, sometimes with the wing attached, sometimes not. During the season, Buddy Baker became the first NASCAR driver to exceed 200 mph posting laps of 200.096 mph and 200.030 mph during test runs at Talladega, in his Daytona.

(ABOVE) **Pete Hamilton one-upped his Superbird teammate, Richard Petty, three times in 1970, winning the Daytona 500 and both of the season's Talladega Superspeedway races.** (TOP) **Richard Petty returned to the Chrysler-Plymouth fold in 1970, driving exotic Plymouth Superbirds.**

The most surprising thing about that season wasn't the thirty-three victories, but the fact that Pete Hamilton, not Richard Petty in his familiar No. 42, won the Daytona 500 and both Talladega races. Hamilton, Petty's teammate, drove No. 70.

Fans loved it. NASCAR, not so much. The old "stinking up the show" rationale resurfaced. NASCAR came down with the hammer on the "winged warriors." For the 1971 season, the "aero cars" (a grouping that included the Ford Torino Talladega and the Mercury Cyclone Spoiler in addition to the Superbird and Daytona), as they were called, were limited to either a 305-cubic-inch (5 L) engine displacement or mandated extra weight. That ended the cars' competitiveness on the racetrack. It also ended the Superbird's days on the production line. The "win on Sunday, sell on Monday" slogan no longer applied.

With the aerodynamic aviary shuttered, the Superbird was history.

(continues on page 94)

Pete Hamilton achieved one of NASCAR's most memorable upsets by winning the 1970 Daytona 500, driving the No. 40 Plymouth Superbird. The No. 43 car of teammate Richard Petty was out with engine problems after only seven laps. Just in case anyone needed convincing, the relatively unknown Hamilton then won both of the season's races at Talladega Superspeedway.

Richard Petty and the No. 43 Superbird may have faltered at Daytona and Talladega in 1970, but that was balanced by eighteen victories overall that season.

ALEXIS LERAS

THERE WILL BE NO ARGUMENT about including this person in these pages. Alexis Leras was a maverick in so many ways, at the beginning. At the end, she was a legend.

She remains so.

How was she an outsider? She was a female to start. And a newspaper reporter to boot. Neither stopped NASCAR President Bill France Jr., from hiring her as a secretary—there were no administrative assistant titles at the time—then promoting her to run public relations.

And run it she did, until leaving NASCAR to handle PR for team owner Harry Melling and superstar-in-the-making Bill Elliott, who for years was the master of the one-word answer to reporters. Leras got Awesome Bill to act a bit less like he was Dawsonville. She got him up to five or six words per response, then actual paragraphs, digging deep to take the good ol' out of the boy for at least a few minutes here and there. She earned a reputation as a serious gatekeeper among media.

"She was the one you wanted to be like," said Danielle Frye, who also handled public relations for both NASCAR and a driver (Dale Jarrett). "I met her when I was like twelve years old. I wanted her job back then."

In 1978, NASCAR shocked the world—or at least the NASCAR fan base—by visiting a Democratic White House. Probably helped that Jimmy Carter was from Georgia. Surely helped that Leras was running the show.

NASCAR's twenty-eight-year string of holding the NASCAR Cup Series Awards show in New York City at the Waldorf Astoria? Leras was in the middle of that too when it began in 1981.

Alexis Leras made being a public relations representative cool, first at NASCAR where she wrangled President Bill France Jr.—no easy task—and then as the PR gatekeeper for NASCAR's longtime most popular driver, Bill Elliott.

She made a difference in big events. Day-to-day NASCAR operations too, like lobbying for an increased female presence in the NASCAR garage. Women weren't allowed into the garage until 1972. She also went above and beyond assisting female media members, cognizant that reception from some competitors and officials might be less than welcoming.

"The word 'trailblazer' gets thrown around a lot but if anybody fits that description it certainly had to be her," said Ken Willis, longtime columnist at the *Daytona Beach News-Journal*, where Leras worked before coming to NASCAR.

Trailblazer, maverick, same deal, right?

"You hear a lot about what the atmosphere and the NASCAR community was back then, when it was male dominated. For her to be able to accomplish all she did and weather the storm we all assumed she had to weather."

Leras, a New York native, grew up in Daytona Beach, graduating from the same school as France, Seabreeze High. She attended Florida State University and, with her degree in English, taught in high school before becoming a reporter. She also sang quite well. Relevancy? Occasionally, she would serve as the national anthem singer before races.

Leras died in 2021 after a brief bout with cancer. She was eighty years old. She is relevant, still.

Leras was the real deal. She even had her own NASCAR trading card.

In 1977, Janet Guthrie became the first woman to race in the Daytona 500.

JANET GUTHRIE

JANET GUTHRIE showed up at the Daytona International Speedway garage in 1977 eager to compete in her first Daytona 500, one of racing's most esteemed events on its biggest stage. A one-time candidate for a NASA job as an astronaut-scientist, Guthrie came to stock car's most elite ranks equipped with an advanced degree in physics and something she'd need more than that formal education: will and determination.

Fortunately, she had both, along with talent, which she was only beginning to hone.

Becoming the first woman to qualify and race in NASCAR's most celebrated event was never her specific goal. Already with an Indy 500 start on her résumé, Guthrie just wanted the chance to race at the highest level, gender be damned. It wasn't a headline seek; it was simply the fundamental next step in her career.

Guthrie had already endured the novelty of competing in the male-dominated sport, making a handful of starts in both open wheel and stock cars before that February Daytona 500 entry. Only three months before Daytona, Guthrie became the first woman to start the Indianapolis 500. And not only did she earn a historic place on the grid, she finished twenty-ninth, retiring early with engine woes, but earning huge respect from the fans. And more tellingly, respect even from some of her competitors.

In 1976, Guthrie became the first woman to compete in NASCAR's elite Cup Series superspeedway race at Charlotte Motor Speedway and then ran her first race on the 2.5-mile Daytona high banks that summer, finishing fifteenth—one of five NASCAR Cup Series events she qualified for that season and a strong inaugural showing on the notoriously intimidating track.

But it was racing in the 1977 Daytona 500 that more firmly put Guthrie on the NASCAR path and further established her as a legitimate competitor. Guthrie finished eighteenth in the Daytona 500 qualifying race, which placed her thirty-ninth on the starting grid; a historic moment. And, for the record, she rolled off a row ahead a then two-time Indy 500 winner Johnny Rutherford, who had missed the show in qualifying but moved on to the grid after another car was disqualified.

A record eighty-two cars had shown up at Daytona International Speedway intent to make the forty-two-car field—the list of those missing out was as nearly as impressive as those who prevailed; a young, future NASCAR Cup Series champion, Hall of Famer, and Daytona 500 winner, Bill Elliott, was among the drivers who failed to make the race that February.

When the Daytona 500 green flag dropped, Guthrie intentionally played a delicate strategy of good pace and careful craft. And it paid off. On a late restart when lined up alongside the legend A. J. Foyt, Guthrie said he looked over toward her, smiled, and waved.

With ten laps remaining, Guthrie had moved her No. 68 Kelly Girl Chevy Chevelle Laguna to a race-best eighth position only to have her car start smoking. She made a quick pit stop then returned to the track, and by her recollection was ninth at the checkered flag. An examination of official timing and scoring relegated her to twelfth. But that was still good enough to make her the top rookie in the Daytona 500.

It was winner, Cale Yarborough, who appeared on the cover of *Sports Illustrated*, however.

Wrecks and engine troubles sidelined more than half the field that day, including Richard Petty, who had publicly questioned Guthrie's legitimacy in a man's sport. He finished twenty-sixth with engine problems.

Petty had been among the most vocal of opponents to Guthrie finding a place in the sport—so much so, she said of their first meeting with NASCAR's King, that his handshake was so cold it felt like she would acquire "frostbite."

Instead, it further motivated Guthrie, who was able to put together enough sponsorship and support to compete in nineteen of the thirty races that season. She finished twelfth or better in ten of those starts, establishing a high mark for a female driver in NASCAR's big leagues that remains the standard today.

She finished sixth in the August 1977 Bristol (Tennessee) Motor Speedway night race, ahead of future NASCAR Hall of Famers, such as Petty and Bobby Allison.

It would be another full thirty-seven years later—another open wheel NASCAR convert—before Danica Patrick would go on to equal Guthrie's best finish, placing sixth in the NASCAR

From 1976 through '80 Janet Guthrie made thirty-three NASCAR Cup Series starts, with five top-ten finishes.

Cup Series race at Atlanta Motor Speedway in 2014, a year after Patrick made history as the first woman to earn pole position in the series in the 2013 Daytona 500.

In between Guthrie and Patrick, a handful of women made NASCAR starts primarily in the support level, overcoming the doubters, trying to show what opportunity can produce.

Although there were certainly hard-knock lessons and bad attitudes during her trailblazing move into auto racing's highest levels, Janet Guthrie prevailed in gumption, in talent, and in results.

She made the difference for generations.

(continues on page 100)

MARTY ROBBINS

Country music star Marty Robbins liked to race too. He was pretty good: six top tens in thirty-five starts. Finished fifth at Michigan. Sounds like a song title.

MARTY ROBBINS, the country and western singing star and part-time NASCAR driver, was also a good friend of NASCAR founder Bill France Sr. A fishing buddy. A free late-night crooner. A teetotaler among those who weren't, especially on some of those fishing trips to places like Walker's Cay in the Bahamas.

"Big Bill" would have Marty and a couple of bandmates flown down to Walker's Cay. Robbins would play the first round of music during the fourth round of drinks. One of France's favorites, "My Way," sounded pretty good with a twang, especially after a few Chivas Regals.

"Like Bill, Marty had two loves, racing stock cars and fishing. I really think music and performing came in third for Marty," the late, former NASCAR executive Jim Foster wrote in an unfinished France biography.

Robbins—Martin David Robinson on his birth (1925) and death (1982) certificates—started playing guitar during his World War II years in the navy. After the war, he kept strumming and started singing too at local clubs and radio stations. Martin David Robinson was doomed, ditched in favor of, first, Jack Robinson and, finally, Marty Robbins.

Hit records followed and, Foster writes, "Moving to Nashville, Tennessee, and the Grand Ole Opry put him close to Nashville Speedway at the fairgrounds. And driving stock cars on a Saturday night was his hobby."

Robbins raced midgets, then modifieds, and finally late models where he started "making a reputation as a stock car driver as well as a country music headliner," Foster writes. "France had seen him race many times at the small NASCAR tracks and was also a big fan of his music. He invited Marty to the Talladega race in 1971 and his band played at the Grand Marshal's dinner the night before. By 1972, Marty had a purple-and-yellow car and was competing in selected Winston Cup races."

Robbins was incredibly popular with NASCAR fans, and his presence at events further strengthened the natural bond between NASCAR and country music.

"I just really enjoy being around these guys," Robbins said toward the end of his racing days. Years before, it was about more than enjoyment.

"This is good business," Robbins told the *Detroit Free Press* in 1974. "The more fans see me race, the more they buy my records. The more they buy my records, the more money I make. What is country and western music? It's Southern music. What is stock car racing? It's Southern racing. It's as simple as that."

Robbins posted what proved to be his best career finish the next day, a fifth at Michigan International Speedway's 2-mile oval, driving a Dodge in the Motor State 360. He made thirty-five NASCAR Cup Series starts between 1966 and 1982 with six top-ten finishes including that one top five.

As a musician, he had better stats.

His single "El Paso City" went to number one. "A White Sport Coat (And a Pink Carnation)" reached number two. Robbins won two Grammy Awards and was inducted into the Country Music Halll of Fame in 1982, the year he died at the age of fifty-seven.

In tune on the high banks: Marty Robbins raced five times at Daytona International Speedway, with a best finish of eighth in the 1974 Firecracker 400.

BILL FRANCE, NASCAR TEAMS GO TO LE MANS

EVEN DECADES AFTER NASCAR established itself as a compelling and staying story in the motorsports scene, the more formal establishment high-nosed the idea of stock cars and stock car drivers competing in the uppity royal sports car landscape of Europe's 24 Hours of Le Mans.

NASCAR founder Bill France, however, was intent to test his style of car and competitor in the world's renowned sports car scene. And in the summer of 1976, France brought over two very "American" entries to go door to door with Europe's best—a Dodge Charger to be driven by Hershel McGriff and his son Doug and a Ford Torino prepared by one of NASCAR's longtime entries, Junie Donlavey, with Richard Brooks and Dick Hutcherson sharing the wheel.

The original idea was to bring the top finisher from France's Rolex 24 sports car race but neither of the top-finishing teams was available, so France asked the Rolex 24 third-place finishers Hershel—who had some road course experience—and his son Doug McGriff. NASCAR picked the second car and chose the owner/driver Donlavey.

The Le Mans opportunity was something France greatly appreciated. Although NASCAR was widely recognized for its oval competition on myriad speedways around the United States, "Big Bill" always kept a soft spot in his heart for road racing. And Le Mans was a place representing both a challenge and an achievement.

France and the Le Mans governing body agreed on a special namesake classification on the grid for the stock cars: the Grand International Class. And it was pleasurably evident that the worldwide sports car race was as excited to host and see NASCAR's entries as NASCAR was to participate.

American racing writer Randy Hallman wrote, "From the moment they arrived in France, the hulking Detroit beasts created a stir, fans flocked around the cars wherever they went. Indeed, they looked as out of place as if they'd been beamed down from some hovering starship—and got almost as much attention."

As the lore goes, race fans and locals began calling the American team and its large stock car entries, "les deux monstres," which meant "the two monsters."

That international attention was good . . . and appreciated. And McGriff and Dunlavey and their teams became a sole fascination for the people crowded into Le Mans. And it was mutually beneficial.

McGriff, who earned four career NASCAR Cup Series wins in 1954, never competed in a full NASCAR season. But his career spanned twenty-nine years—from his first start in 1950 at Darlington, South Carolina, to his final on the Sonoma, California, road course in 1993 at the age of sixty-five. He and his thirty-year-old son Doug became racing sensations, unlike anything they had experienced back in America.

The same was true for Dunlavey, a NASCAR stalwart already in the stock car scene. His co-driver at Le Mans, Hutcherson, was a proven endurance competitor; in fact, he was part of the Ford team that beat Ferrari at Le Mans in 1966.

McGriff qualified his Dodge Charger forty-seventh fastest. And Dunlavey's co-driver, Dick Hutcherson, qualified their Ford Torino fifty-fifth—the last position on the historic Le Mans grid.

BILL FRANCE'S SON, BILL FRANCE JR., waved the green flag to start that 1976 race. But unfortunately, a mere two laps later, McGriff's Charger lost its engine. The Torino made it into the night, finally retiring eleven hours in.

Their finish is not the whole story however, not even really the compelling part of the story. NASCAR had proven itself every bit up to the nod of classic motorsports, popular, intriguing, and full of that spirit that eventually formed a true bond—felt even today—with the iconic Le Mans event and the up-for-anything NASCAR, even forty-eight years later with its most recent Le Mans entry, the 2023 Garage 56.

Even though neither of the NASCAR teams was part of a victory celebration in 1976, McGriff recalled and appreciated the scene very well; summing up and foretelling automotive journalist Matt Stone, "I love the end of that race. People go crazy. They flood the grandstands. They drink . . .

"Vive la France, y'all."

Hershel McGriff and his son, Doug, brought a Dodge Charger to the 1976 24 Hours of Le Mans, part of a two-car NASCAR-based contingent arranged by NASCAR President Bill France Sr. Here, Hershel races under the Dunlop Bridge.

NASCAR Cup Series team owner Junie Donlavey brought a NASCAR-style Ford Torino to the 1976 24 Hours of Le Mans. Donlavey coaxed Dick Hutcherson out of retirement to co-drive the car with Dick Brooks and Frenchman Marcel Mignot.

"THE FIGHT": 1979 DAYTONA 500

FOR SO MANY, the most iconic photographs of the 1979 Daytona 500 aren't of a dramatic finish at the line, but of the fisticuffs happening in Turns 3 and 4 among three future NASCAR Hall of Famers.

That 1979 Daytona 500 was the first NASCAR race of any kind to appear "flag to flag" on national network television and it did not disappoint. In fact, it couldn't have been more must-see viewing for stock car fans already in love with the sport or the thousands of potential new fans watching a compelling sporting drama unfold via CBS live broadcast.

A competitive dustup on track battling for the lead on the last lap of The Great American Race between Cale Yarborough and Donnie Allison wrecked both cars and left the two drivers emerging to take matters into their own hands.

Meanwhile, less than a mile away from the infield spectacle, NASCAR's perennial superstar Richard Petty cruised to the checkered flag to win his sixth of a career total of seven Daytona 500s by a car length over another soon-to-be NASCAR Hall of Famer Darrell Waltrip and racing icon A. J. Foyt, another two car lengths back in third.

The finish to that race on track may have historical significance, but it was the action off track that seared the sport into mainstream consciousness.

Donnie Allison and Yarborough climbed from their wrecked cars and had pointed words for one another as Bobby Allison drove down into the grassy infield to offer his younger brother, Donnie, a ride back to the garage. By that time, finger pointing quickly had turned into a wrestling match: the Allison brothers versus Yarborough—all the drama caught on live television and saved in photographs that remain forever a part of NASCAR lore.

The first two to make contact were actually Yarbrough and Bobby Allison (still in his car at that point), stemming from issues between them earlier in the race. Once those two were out and swinging, Donnie joined in and it was all track marshals could do to separate the men. To this day, Bobby Allison smiles and insists that Cale "was trying to hit Bobby's fist with his nose."

"It seems absolutely crazy," 2012 NASCAR Cup Series champion Brad Keselowski said of that historical race. "It's hard for me to put in context intelligently something that happened before I was born, but my impressions of that moment were that it was kind of the perfect storm in so many cliché ways with respect to so many fans watching, it being the biggest race of the year, and the emotion behind it.

"I've heard so much about it and it continues to endure and I think that's one of the rare moments in time."

The three main players, the late Yarborough and the Allison brothers, would field questions about that race more than anything else they accomplished in their careers, long after hanging up their driving shoes. Which is saying a lot, considering Yarborough won three consecutive NASCAR Cup Series championships and eighty-three races. His five wins in the Daytona 500 is second only to Petty's seven.

Bobby Allison won the 1983 championship and claimed eighty-four trophies—three of them Daytona 500 victories, including the last win of his career in 1988. And his brother, Donnie, won ten races and will be inducted into the 2024 Class of the NASCAR Hall of Fame joining his brother and Yarborough.

In later years, long out of the cockpit, the three drivers could smile about that important part of NASCAR history. But, perhaps most telling, they still did not agree on what led up to one of the—unintentionally—most significant moments in their sport's history.

These mavericks defined an era and pioneered a passion that remains today.

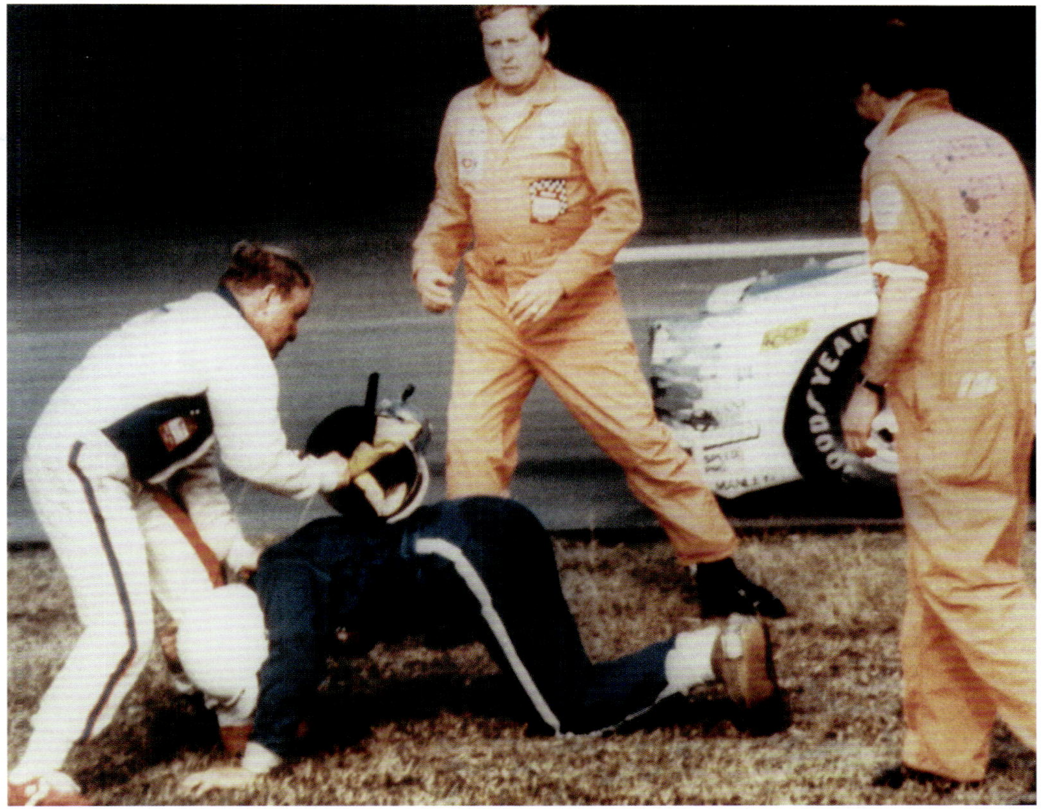

(ABOVE AND OPPOSITE) **The 1979 Daytona 500 ended with a lap 199 crash involving Donnie Allison and Cale Yarborough. They climbed out of their wrecked cars to discuss matters, and Donnie's brother Bobby showed up. All hell broke loose.**

Havoline
28
12
BUICK
DieHard
Stewart

CHAPTER 5

THE 1980s

STARS, SPEEDS, AND SAFETY CONCERNS

A highlight of this decade dealt with pure speed as the ultimate qualifying record of 212 mph was set by Bill Elliott at Talladega in 1987. During that race, a car nearly went into the grandstands, leading NASCAR to institute a carburetor restrictor plate to slow the cars to a safer speed on the larger speedways. This move opened myriad opportunities for inventive engineers to circumvent the new rule. It was a golden opportunity for the "mavericks," among them Elliott's brother, Ernie.

ANOTHER BIG CHANGE during this decade was the fact that the drivers were becoming very media savvy. Outspoken Darrell Waltrip led the charge. No longer was bad grammar or thick accents the norm. Drivers found themselves representing the sport on national television shows and were official representatives of their sponsors. Drivers were more aware of their general appearance both on and off the track, and many hired managers to coordinate their public appearances and media opportunities.

Another important chapter of the '80s was the emergence of a larger-than-life everyman, Dale Earnhardt. His fierce driving style brought him scores of fans and gave him legendary status while still competing. Also, "The King" Richard Petty, a seven-time champion, scored his seventh Daytona 500 win.

Road racing was in the NASCAR mix as California's Riverside Raceway closed after many years. But the stock cars came back to the scenic Watkins Glen International in the winemaking region of New York and also to the wine country of Sonoma, California, with new road racing stars such as Tim Richmond and Ricky Rudd emerging.

(PREVIOUS) **Bobby Allison (12) leads his son Davey Allison (28) during the 1988 Daytona 500. Father-son finished 1-2; it was Bobby's last victory as several months later he barely survived a career-ending crash at Pocono Raceway.**

DALE EARNHARDT

DALE EARNHARDT. The Intimidator. A maverick for certain, Dale Earnhardt was also a change agent.

He altered NASCAR Cup Series racing, making intimidation a key element to reaching Victory Lane, especially when accented by some late-lap bumper car tactics. And because of that, he stood as both hero and villain to NASCAR followers for most of his twenty-six-year (1975–2000) career.

That's right. Before he died in a Turn 4 wreck on the last lap of the 2001 season-opening Daytona 500, support for Earnhardt was far from universal. You either loved him or loved to hate him, as the old line goes. Like Earnhardt cared.

"He liked to rough you up," said his friend and rival, three-time NASCAR Cup Series champion Darrell Waltrip. "I'd be racing with him and I'd get in front and be looking in the mirror and I'd say, 'Whoops, that was a bad mistake,' because now he's behind me. Never knew where he was going. He didn't necessarily have to have the fastest car . . . he was such a good driver that he could take a mediocre car and get the most out of it and, sometimes, you were the victim . . . that's just who he was and I think he thrived on that."

Earnhardt embodied the everyman image that connected him with so many fans. Impressed by no one, starting with himself, the well-worn word "hardscrabble" is a perfect fit for where he came from . . . he came from nothing, born and raised in the mill town of Kannapolis, North Carolina. His father, Ralph, was one of NASCAR's greatest short track drivers. Ralph raced to win—and to put food on the table for his family. Dale came into stock car racing with the same immediate goals.

Dale Earnhardt—you could identify with him. And so, as his career advanced, his fan base increased. Earnhardt fans not only had a hero, they also had a champion. A seven-time champion, tied with Richard Petty for the all-time record, until 2016 when Jimmie Johnson made it a trio.

He left us February 18, 2001, having changed the sport in a variety of ways.

Start with style.

"Dale drove on the superspeedways as if they were short tracks," journalist and author Jonathan Ingram said. "And it took an enormous amount of guts in terms of just physically being not afraid of what might go wrong. And it took a lot of stubbornness when it came to criticism, which he got a lot of."

The classic Intimidator pose. It worked.

In 1979 and 1980, Earnhardt's cars—owned by Rod Osterland—didn't look as menacing as the black No. 3s that were to come. Looks were deceiving. Earnhardt was the Cup Series' rookie of the year in '79; he won the first of seven series championship in '80. In retrospect, a major warning shot.

1986. The No. 2s had been replaced by the eventually-iconic No. 3s. GM Goodwrench-sponsored black cars were still two years away, but the Wrangler rides were fast and Earnhardt was perfecting his take-no-prisoners style that fans either loved or hated. Earnhardt, in his third year with team owner Richard Childress, won his second series championship. And one more thing regarding that Wrangler sponsorship: Who doesn't love a good pair of blue jeans? Ask Dale Jr.

But, as former sportswriter for the *Charlotte Observer* and the *Washington Post*, Liz Clarke adds, "He wasn't a bull in a China shop. I do think, as people would say, that he could wreck people on a superspeedway without ever touching them, by disrupting the air, and I'm sure he put a bumper to people—but there's a calculus in that . . . there were so many ingredients to his mastery at superspeedway racing."

Former *Baltimore Sun* journalist Sandy McKee spent years writing about Earnhardt and a prime subject was the Earnhardt approach. She remembers a classic Buddy Baker synopsis trying to explain what made Earnhardt so tough: "He can see air!" Buddy proclaimed.

From McKee: "Earnhardt told me, with that mischievous grin we were all so used to seeing, 'I can't see air. But, I do know what to do with it.' Seeing air certainly was a mystic ability. It might now be called a superpower. And certainly that was part of [his success] but I think the really big thing that mattered was Dale. His intensity and his desire to win. I heard comments like that from a lot of his fellow competitors, some of whom complained about his 'roughhouse, risky driving,' and others, who recognized it for what it was."

Completing this impromptu media panel is *Autoweek*'s Al Pearce, the dean of NASCAR reporters, having covered his fifty-fifth consecutive Daytona 500 in 2024.

Said Pearce, "I think he brought more intelligence to superspeedway racing, more than anybody ever noticed at the time. You look back on it, after that last race he won [at Talladega, July 2000], and you remember that he was way back and then, all of a sudden, he was in the front, and you don't remember him doing anything extraordinary to get to the front. He just did it."

He just did it off track as well. Dale Earnhardt—The Intimidator—became the definitive NASCAR brand for drivers. *Gentlemen start your merchandise haulers.* Many credit Earnhardt's wife, Teresa, with driving the business, which was run by the astute Don Hawk. Damned if drivers weren't chasing Earnhardt again.

"I think Dale did things that were in other people's worlds, that he put his own spin on," NASCAR Vice Chairman Mike Helton said. "His business acumen . . . for someone who did not have a big formal education, he had his street smarts and common sense. He could see things and then figure out how to make it work. Brilliant."

Praise the Lord and pass the trophy. NASCAR Chaplain "Preacher" Bill Baird chats with driver Dale Earnhardt prior to the running of the Nashville Busch 420 NASCAR Cup race at Nashville Speedway. Baird doesn't look like he's trying to lead Earnhardt in prayer, but his advice might've helped. Earnhardt won the race. He does look skeptical, though, of whatever Baird was saying.

Earnhardt wore a good tux, but probably not that often. It was part of the deal at the NASCAR Cup Series Awards show, for years held at the posh Waldorf-Astoria in New York. Earnhardt is posing with the championship trophy and the quite-cool Goodyear Gold Car Award. Winston sponsored the series then, in case you can't tell from this photo.

Helton was NASCAR's president when Earnhardt died. He oversaw the myriad safety advancements instituted after Earnhardt's death, starting with the HANS (Head and Neck Restraint System) device. *After* is the key word, and a reality that has haunted NASCAR. In 2000, three national series drivers died due to basilar skull fracture, the injury that killed Earnhardt. Entering the 2024 season, *no* national series drivers had died post-Earnhardt.

"The evolution of what we did [concerning safety] after 2001 was accelerated, certainly," Helton will tell you, solemnly. He and Earnhardt were close friends. For Helton, Earnhardt's death was personal.

Earnhardt changed the sport forever when he died. Sad but true.

"With all the milestones that Dale accomplished as a driver and as a person, I don't think that will be his main recognition," Helton said, "but that day we lost him certainly was a [dark] day for NASCAR."

Enough of death. Earnhardt lived a large life, leaving virtually everyone in the NASCAR industry with a story or three. Russell Branham, public relations director for Darlington Raceway, has one of the best you'll hear.

1998. Earnhardt brought his two new Dale Earnhardt Incorporated (DEI) drivers, his son, Dale Jr., and Ron Hornaday, to Darlington, to scope out the treacherous egg-shaped oval. Earnhardt told Branham to get his own car, albeit a company vehicle, for the ridearound.

"It was a Pontiac Bonneville," Branham said. "He hopped in the front passenger seat, Junior and Hornaday got in the back, and he told me to drive. So, I'm going about eighty miles an hour around and he's mad as hell because I'm driving too slow. So I get it up to one hundred fifteen, the tires are squealing. Junior and Hornaday are moving toward the center of the back seat. But now he doesn't like the line. He says, 'You can't drive worth a damn. Move your foot.'"

Branham did and Earnhardt slid over to the left, stretched his left leg and started using his left foot to operate the brake and gas while driving with his right hand, going as fast as the Bonneville would go, half the time looking into the backseat, talking to his guys, taking them to school.

"It was unbelievable," Branham said.

"For him, that was like a Sunday afternoon drive in the country."

(continues on page 112)

Dale Earnhardt's No. 3 Goodwrench Chevrolet that he drove for owner Richard Childress in winning six of his seven NASCAR Cup Series championships. NASCAR's most iconic ride? Has to be between Earnhardt's No. 3 and Richard Petty's No. 43.

L. W. WRIGHT

GOOGLE "L. W. WRIGHT" and he comes right up, with the heading American Con Artist. As if it was a career.

Then again . . . guess it was.

Wright has been part of NASCAR lore since the May 1982 Winston 500. Wright bought a race car and other equipment with bad checks, showed up at Talladega Superspeedway and said he had sponsorship from several country music stars, fabricated a racing background—remarkably qualified for the race—and finished next to last after NASCAR parked him for failing to maintain minimum speed.

Whereupon Wright took off, left his car at Talladega, and vanished.

Two of the people scammed by Wright were NASCAR notables, drivers Coo Coo Marlin and his son, Sterling. The Marlins sold Wright a car; he paid mostly in cash, a check for the rest. The Marlins got the car back—Sterling had to find an old barn outside Nashville that belonged to a friend of Wright and "steal it back"—but the $3,700, it vanished too.

"I knew something funny was going on," Sterling, a future two-time Daytona 500 champion, said in '82. "He was afraid to get into the race car [at the track]."

NASCAR itself fell victim, left holding worthless checks totaling about $1,500 for a competitor's license and pit crew passes. Goodyear got burned for racing tires. And then there was the Nashville businessman who shelled out the original forty-or-so grand that helped buy the race car. Stiffed, as well.

"He was as slippery as a minnow in a bucket," recalled Larry Woody, the former longtime sportswriter at the *Tennessean*, in Nashville. "The whole thing is fascinating, just a really intriguing story . . . If he could have driven as fast as he talked, L. W. Wright would be a NASCAR champion now."

In '82, Woody followed the Wright story as far as he could. For Woody, for everyone, the story ended at 'Dega.

Gone but not forgotten, Wright—real first name Larry—resurfaced in May 2022, on the *Scene Vault Podcast*, interviewed by veteran motorsports journalist Rick Houston, who had been on the hunt for Wright, and his story, for a while.

Interview aside, the mystery continued, fueled by some fans of the popular podcast. Was this really Wright? Woody said he's "ninety-nine point nine percent sure" the old guy showing off an L. W. Wright racing jacket on camera was, indeed, L. W. Wright. Sterling Marlin also saw the podcast and then saw red, again. Old Sterlin' probably felt like going Elvis on the TV. Anyway, another confirmation for Houston's work.

Houston, former reporter at *Winston Cup Scene* magazine, is in the process of digitizing all those old issues to preserve an important part of NASCAR history. One day, the project led him to an old photo of L. W.

"Something just clicked, one thing led to another and I finally found him," said Houston, who is working on a documentary on Wright.

"And yeah, it was him. I'm very satisfied [of that]."

In February 2023, Wright was arrested on various charges that encompassed several states—of course, he was—over a number of years. Say what you will, but L. W. stayed busy. The Tennessee Department of Corrections has him down for twenty-three felonies during his presumably wild-as-hell existence. Once again: a maverick, this time for better or worse.

On January 26, 2024, Wright died at Lois M. DeBerry Special Needs Facility in Nashville, Tennessee, at the age of seventy-six. He had been imprisoned since his arrest.

(THIS PAGE) **The "D. B. Cooper of NASCAR" finally resurfaced in 2022, forty years after he fenagled his way into a Talladega starting spot in the Winston 500, and was parked for going too slow—then disappeared. What a con. Photograph courtesy of Rick Houston/*The Scene Vault Podcast***

(OPPOSITE) **Somewhere back in the pack of the Winston 500 on May 2, 1982, at Talladega Superspeedway is L. W. Wright—maybe. L. W.'s Chevrolet left the race after only thirteen laps, hauling ass, never to be seen by NASCAR types again. Not sure if he was still runnin' when this shot was taken—probably not.**

WINSTON 500

Tim Richmond joined Rick Hendrick's newly formed NASCAR team for the 1986 season. It proved to be a rockin' year as Richmond rolled up seven victories on his way to third overall in that year's Cup series.

TIM RICHMOND

TIM RICHMOND and his comet-like NASCAR career once helped inspire a major motion picture, and that's how his life played out—like a movie. With a tragic ending.

When one looks back, the whole thing seems surreal, Richmond coming from the IndyCar Series to emerge as a NASCAR superstar. Make that rock star, because that's what he was. Racing fast and living faster. It was the 1980s. Guess it couldn't last.

Also surreal was Richmond's death in August 1989, at the age of thirty-four, from complications due to the AIDS virus, a reality that was avoided publicly as long as possible by Richmond, his family, and his sport.

But before that finality in a West Palm Beach, Florida, hospital, there were eight magical seasons. Eight seasons—1980 to '87—and thirteen victories. That's all it took for immortality. NASCAR named him one of its Fifty Greatest Drivers in '88.

And that he was, surely, as he brought raw talent like few had seen before, to NASCAR, especially adept at road courses—and messing with Dale Earnhardt. Richmond could rock 'n' roll with The Intimidator. He knew it. Earnhardt knew it. Fans loved it.

Fans loved Richmond, period, with his long hair, loud talk, and larger-than-life persona. NASCAR's most renowned promoter, former Charlotte Motor Speedway President Humpy Wheeler, embraced the Richmond phenomenon. "We've never had a race driver like Tim in stock car racing," Wheeler said. "He was almost a James Dean–like character."

Live fast, die young, leave a good-looking corpse—a quote mainly attributable to the famous actor—fit Richmond's existence like a glove.

The living part—more about that, right?

Richmond was the racer that *Days of Thunder* character Cole Trickle, played by Tom Cruise, was more or less based upon: open wheel up-and-comer, ignorant of a stock car's handling intricacies, a foot-to-the-floor kind of guy.

He mashed the gas in 1986, his final full season and his best one: seven victories, eight poles, thirteen top-five finishes, and seventeen top tens. A career-best third in the final Cup Series standings. In Richmond and Hendrick Motorsports' No. 25 Chevrolet sponsored by Folger's, NASCAR had two icons in the making, one man, one car—the Folger's Coffee Machine, as the bright-red ride came to be called. Championships were on deck, or at least it seemed.

Just as suddenly, it started unraveling. In December 1986, Richmond became ill and ended up missing the Daytona 500 two months later. The illness was officially reported as pneumonia. Media reports started indicating it was AIDS.

Richmond returned to the track in the summer of '87 and remarkably won back-to-back races at Pocono Raceway and Riverside.

"Can you think of another athlete in history who knows they're going to die and they're performing at that level," said Jeff Snook, the *Palm Beach Post* reporter who broke the news about Richmond having AIDS.

Snook is from Richmond's hometown of Ashland, Ohio, but he's not a fan because of what he calls post-diagnosis irresponsible behavior. But that doesn't erase the obvious.

"Tim had all the skill, all the talent in the world," Snook said.

In the years since his death, revisionists have pondered what might have been. Often, it's the championships Dale Earnhardt won, rather than the ones Richmond didn't, that crop up.

"I may make a lot of enemies saying this, but I am not so sure Dale Earnhardt would have dominated the sport the way he did if Richmond had been around . . . Richmond had more talent in his little finger than the rest of us ever had, period," Kyle Petty told author David Poole for his Richmond biography, *Tim Richmond: The Fast Life and Remarkable Times of NASCAR's Top Gun.*

After his back-to-back triumphs, Richmond raced six more times during the 1987 season before resigning from the Hendrick team in September. Richmond wanted to attempt a comeback in '88 but was suspended by NASCAR for failing a drug test. Richmond was retested and reinstated later that season but there were no rides available. Had to be the damaged goods theory. Richmond sued NASCAR regarding his suspension and the case was settled out of court.

With no racing in sight, Richmond went home, to die.

(continues on page 116)

Tim Richmond made Hendrick Motorsports' Folger's-sponsored Chevrolet iconic, forever known as the "Folger's Coffee Machine."

Tim Richmond was somewhat popular during his NASCAR heyday. Turned out to be the good news and the bad news.

GARY NELSON

WHEN NASCAR HIRED GARY NELSON as the NASCAR Winston Cup Series Director in 1991, the sport tilted on its Southeastern axis. The man was generally regarded as, if not the biggest, certainly the slickest cheater in NASCAR history, a view reinforced by Nelson himself who will always remind you that he "never got penalized."

Which translated to this: Overnight, the landscape of the NASCAR garage area had changed forever. Competitors knew it. Things, finally, were gonna get tight. Nelson would make sure.

Reactions followed a common theme, somewhere between faked outrage and bemusement. They were funny then, as they are now.

Famous quote, if not an original one, from Darrell Waltrip: "This is like letting one of the inmates run the asylum."

Nationally syndicated columnist Paul Harvey didn't know the rest of *this* story, but that didn't stop him from writing about Nelson's hiring. That's right. Paul Harvey, on NASCAR.

"Nelson is one of the best cheaters motorsports has ever produced," Harvey wrote in a 1992 piece. "The theory is that you hire a thief to catch a thief . . . NASCAR has appointed one tough 'top cop' to snoopervise infractions."

Yes, snoopervise. NASCAR's version of Le Mans' scrutineering, apparently.

Funny story about how Nelson ended up at NASCAR. Upset about getting a small fine for what he deemed a bogus infraction, and mad about NASCAR officiating in general, Nelson vented to a journalist in the summer of 1988, detailing many of his technical "innovations" through the years, starting in '81 as Bobby Allison's crew chief. Not long after the piece published, NASCAR President Bill France Jr. offered Nelson a job as an official working under then-Cup Director Dick Beaty. Nelson declined several times, until '91.

As a crew chief, Nelson saw opportunities in terms of both the rulebook and the people enforcing the rules. "I spent a lot of time looking at what guys were doing, and I spent a lot of time looking at what the officials were checking and that gave us our windows of opportunity," Nelson said in 2024. "It was like, 'If those guys are getting away with it, we should do it. And if the officials aren't looking at this other part, we should work on that.'

"Into the early eighties, even though it was the Cup Series, the technical people were not race car savvy . . . so that's where we were able to find advantages, or at least ways to stay even. I was always on pins and needles that we were going to get caught for something and get kicked out. But it didn't happen my whole career."

Miracle.

In 1982, the rear bumper of Bobby Allison's car fell off during the Daytona 500. That never happened, the cars were so sturdy. Allison, driving a considerably lighter car, went on to win NASCAR's biggest race. In '95, Greg Sacks drove a research and development car prepared by Nelson to a major upset victory at the Pepsi 400. After that victory, Nelson returned the car to the shop—permanently. Hmmm. And then there was the matter of fuel mileage. Nelson-wrenched rides sure seemed to have a regular leg up there, as well.

You get the idea why NASCAR wanted this guy on their side.

Which Nelson was, big-time, moving from Winston Cup director to vice president of research and development. First job coinciding with the aftermath of Dale Earnhardt's deadly crash at the 2001 Daytona 500: Build a safer car.

Nelson and his team did it. Called it the Car of Tomorrow. Drivers didn't like it. Neither did manufacturers or fans. Cosmetically, it wasn't a beauty, but combined with the advent of SAFER barriers and the HANS device, it solidified a new wave of safety emphasis, unlike anything before. Earnhardt died on February 18, 2001. As of the start of the 2024 season, no drivers had died in a NASCAR national series since that dark day. Nelson is proud of that, as anyone who cares one whit about NASCAR should be.

Nelson left NASCAR in 2007 and moved into a managerial role with the successful International Motor Sports Association team, Action Express. A new legacy is being built, or at least an addendum to the original, which was both colorful and monumental.

Gary Nelson, in the formative cheatin' years.

Gary Nelson, one of all-time greatest rule breakers in NASCAR, became the NASCAR Cup Series director in 1991.

THE ALABAMA GANG

IN A SPORT founded upon and replete of legend, "The Alabama Gang" of drivers and champions has endured and excelled—their competitive contributions came a generation ago yet their presence and legacy remain a forever integral part of NASCAR's lore.

Although the Allison family of NASCAR Hall of Famer brothers Bobby and Donnie actually started their careers from their native Miami, their more commanding rise to fame came after a move closer to the heart of stock cars, to Hueytown, Alabama. There they cultivated a lifelong friendship with gentleman racer Red Farmer and another Alabama driver, NASCAR star Neil Bonnett.

The quartet, which quickly became known as "The Alabama Gang," were as tight off track as they were competitive on track and, for all intents and purposes, Alabama's answer to the more traditional North Carolinian brand of the sport's elite.

In stock cars, Farmer, who is now ninety-one years old, made only thirty-six NASCAR Cup Series starts—his career best a pair of top-five finishes at nearby Macon, Georgia. And his "home" Talladega (Alabama) Superspeedway. At the age of fifty-five, he won in the ARCA Menards Series driving for Bobby's son, the late Davey Allison—and, none too surprisingly, both his ARCA wins came on his hometown Talladega high banks. It is estimated that Farmer has won more than nine hundred races, the bulk being dirt late-model competitions, where he was competing locally in his late eighties and winning races in his seventies.

From left, **Neil Bonnett, Donnie Allison, and Bobby Allison, members of the famed "Alabama Gang."**

Farmer is both universally beloved in the sport and respected for a longevity of success perhaps never to be seen again; a maverick in a sport that cultivated the exceptional.

Bonnett, a Hueytown native, was a familiar name to NASCAR fans from his excellence on track to his ease in front of the television cameras sharing tales of the sport from on track, in garage, and the comfy confines of the racers' homes and haunts. His and Farmer's friendship with the Allisons drew the families to the Alabama base.

Competitively, Bonnett won eighteen NASCAR Cup Series races between 1977 and '88, driving for some of the sport's greatest teams such as the Wood Brothers and Junior Johnson.

But he was also well known as one of the late Dale Earnhardt's best friends; making a name for himself on television with his down-home charm and fun personality—always up for whatever lay ahead. He once famously crashed out early in a race then went up to the CBS broadcast booth to call the rest of the event for the television audience.

After recovering from a severe crash in 1990, Bonnett went on to be a respected contributor to TNN and TBS Sports NASCAR coverage, and even earned legitimate acting parts in the hugely popular *Days of Thunder* and *Stroker Ace* movies.

But drawn back to the racetrack in 1994 for another shot at Daytona 500 glory, Bonnett, forty-seven, was tragically killed in a racing accident during opening practice.

It was part of what became an unbelievable linkage of triumph and tragedy among these four legendary competitors and their families. Their names and legends provided a simultaneous and equal-parts dose of heart warmth and heartbreak—even today, representing so much good in the sport during a wave of national popularity for NASCAR.

Donnie Allison, eighty-four, named to the 2024 NASCAR Hall of Fame Class, will join his older brother, Bobby, in that rarefied consideration. Allison had success in the NASCAR premier ranks, winning ten races, including two at "The Alabama Gang's" Talladega home track (in 1971 and '77). He famously sparred with Cale Yarborough in the Daytona International Speedway infield during that 1979 Daytona 500 national television debut. He's been a steady ambassador for NASCAR ever since.

But unquestionably, it was Bobby Allison, now eighty-six, who is most synonymous with The Alabama Gang; his excellence on track and the emotional toils away from the track have forever been a symbol of strength and uncommon bravery.

Red Farmer (*right*) celebrates in Victory Lane at Talladega Superspeedway with his car owner Davey Allison after Farmer won the ARCA Permatex 500K in 1988. They were also together in July 1993 at the same track, in a helicopter crash that killed Allison.

He enjoyed some of the sport's biggest victories and absolutely endured great tragedy.

Bobby Allison's work behind the steering wheel resulted in eighty-four trophies, tying him with Darrell Waltrip for fourth most all-time in the sport—and included a showstopping victory in his final Daytona 500 at the age of forty-nine. That 1988 race remains of one of the most memorable in NASCAR history, with Bobby holding off his twenty-six-year-old son Davey to claim his third Daytona 500 victory . . . and Bonnett coming home a strong fourth place.

It was a transformational moment for "The Alabama Gang," with the promising next generation featuring Davey and his younger brother, Clifford, who seemed primed to follow in their father Bobby's illustrious footsteps. But unfathomably, the talented next generation never got a real chance to show its massive possibilities.

Bobby Allison (*right*) celebrates his 1988 Daytona 500 victory with his son Davey, who finished second. It was Bobby's last victory, as his career was ended several months later by a bad crash at Pocono Raceway.

Davey, thirty-two, was killed in a helicopter accident at the beloved Talladega track in 1993, less than a year after his younger brother, Clifford, twenty-seven, lost his life in an accident during a NASCAR Busch Series practice session at Michigan International Speedway and months before Bonnett would perish at Daytona.

As with the massive glory "The Alabama Gang" earned, the tragedy they endured is very much a part of the story of this group of massively talented friends that forged a brotherhood of generations.

Farmer, Bonnett, and the Allison family were true mavericks for their work in the sport. Their accomplishments, must-know history, and their competitive gifts still appreciated in the decades since.

The originators, not the imitators. The "official" Alabama Gang poses here at a NASCAR race: (from left) Bobby Allison, Donnie Allison, and Charles "Red" Farmer. Don't let the old folks' smiles fool you. These Southern Gentlemen are bad-asses to their core.

"The Alabama Gang" is a rich chapter of NASCAR's history: Immensely talented racers earning NASCAR Hall of Fame status while earning the respect of competitors and the love of fans.

Transformational mavericks, whose work behind the wheel as hugely talented competitors has been matched with a special adoration and respect that remains fundamental to their contribution to the sport.

(continues on page 122)

FORD THUNDERBIRD

IN THE NASCAR GARAGE, they called the car the "football" due to its rounder-than-ever aerodynamics and slightly smaller size. Maybe a better nickname was the "speeding bullet."

The latest and greatest Ford Thunderbirds in 1983 looked fast just sitting there, as the old garage speak goes. They were unique, with implications beyond the racetrack, just like the good ol' days that were quickly getting older, those days of tangible links between 200-mile-per-hour NASCAR Cup Series cars and sedans stuck in traffic—drafting at 5 miles per hour—on Interstate 4 trying to get into the Daytona 500.

Concurrent with the repercussions in NASCAR, the new Thunderbird design would soon lend itself to the Ford Taurus, one of the most popular passenger sedans of all time. Footballs, road, and track.

Thunderbirds won fifty-three NASCAR Cup Series races in the 1980s. None wining more races (thirty-two in the decade) or bigger races than Bill Elliott's 'Birds. Other wheelmen in T-Birds were Cale Yarborough, Kyle Petty, Ricky Rudd, Buddy Baker, Mark Martin, and Davey Allison. But Elliott, a shy, red-haired, soft-spoken Georgian, became synonymous with the Thunderbird, specifically the No. 9 red-white-and-gold Coors Thunderbird, destined to evolve into one of NASCAR's most iconic cars.

In 1985, Elliott went faster than anymore had before, posting qualifying records at 2.5-mile Daytona International Speedway (210.364 mph) and 2.66-mile Talladega Superspeedway (212.809 mph). As of 2024, those records still stood. Might as well be 2054. The advent of carburetor (and, later, fuel injection) restrictions in 1988 ensured slower speeds at NASCAR's two biggest tracks—and ensured Elliott would forever hold the records.

Elliott also won the "Winston Million" bonus in '85 via victories in the Daytona 500, the Winston 500 at Talladega, and the Southern 500 at Darlington Raceway. That amounted to three of what series sponsor R. J. Reynolds designated as the Cup Series' four major races. Cool promotion, provided tobacco advertising didn't offend you. The lineup was the richest race (Daytona), the fastest (Winston 500), the longest (Coca-Cola 600 at Charlotte Motor Speedway), and the oldest (Southern 500.) Winning at least three of the four got you the million bucks.

It also got Elliott a second nickname. He already was being called "awesome Bill from Dawsonville" but now fans had to make room in their vernacular for "Million Dollar Bill."

"Bill Elliott's car was the epitome of craftsmanship and what a football shape does for you," said Jeff Hammond, crew chief for Darrell Waltrip's championship seasons in 1982 and '85. "That little car would haul the mail."

Strange side note: Elliott won eleven races in '85, one of best seasons in Cup Series history. NASCAR's point system, heavily emphasizing consistency over the course of the then twenty-race season, awarded the championship to Waltrip.

Nonetheless, Elliott—who went on to win his only Cup title in 1988—had his spectacular season and an extra million. Thanks in large part to a special ride.

"Well, I often said when Ford came out with the T-Bird it was a very aerodynamic car, and I think we kind of understood it very well," Elliott told *RACER* magazine after he retired from driving. "And that helped lead us to the things that we did as far as the car goes. . .

"Those Thunderbirds were something different than what we were used to seeing. And they were something that helped mold the sport."

(THIS PAGE) **The fastest car in NASCAR history—and one of the most popular, the Coors Ford Thunderbird.**

(OPPOSITE) **At the 1987 Winston 500, Bill Elliott, driving the No. 9 Coors Ford Thunderbird, topped qualifying on the 2.66-mile tri-oval with a 212.809 mph lap, fastest in NASCAR history. Hence, the cheesy signage!**

TALLADEGA USA
BUSCH
MELLING
OIL PUMPS
9
WORLD'S
FASTEST
RACE CAR

DARRELL WALTRIP

UPON FURTHER review, it appears Darrell Waltrip was the right man for the right time in NASCAR.

"You nailed it," Waltrip said this year, of that assessment. The subject was those other years, *his* years—the late 1970s and early '80s when he was winning races and championships and causing a ruckus along the way.

"Jaws" was the nickname attached to Waltrip. Heated rival Cale Yarborough called him that after a multicar crash in the 1977 Southern 500 took them both out of the race. The movie *Jaws* about the killer shark was a big hit. So was the nickname.

Darrell Waltrip was a fast talker and a faster driver. The man they called "Jaws" became a three-time NASCAR Cup Series champion. Nice hair, as well, especially early in his career.

It stuck, as did the comparison to another brash talker, Muhammad Ali, who wasn't universally popular in the good ol' NASCAR garages.

"It took a great deal of gumption," former Charlotte Motor Speedway President Humpy Wheeler said.

"I think Darrell was a creation," said veteran *Autoweek* journalist Al Pearce. "It was kind of like 'Look at me, I'm cute, I'm clever, I've got my wife [Stevie] with me, my hair is just so.'"

Waltrip had much to talk about. He won eighty-four races, tied for fourth all-timer with Bobby Allison—and NASCAR Cup Series championships in 1981, '82, and '85. He won twenty-seven times before any Cup championships. Starting in '81, Junior Johnson hired him to drive. They knew what was coming, even if no one else did: one of the greatest runs in Cup history.

With Johnson, there was less jawing. "He set me down one day and said, 'Listen, boy, I'll do the talkin' and you do the drivin', and when Junior Johnson talked, you listened," Waltrip said. "And then we won the lottery."

NASCAR's equivalent for sure. Those twenty-seven previous trips to Victory Lane were almost dwarfed by the partnership: They won forty-three more in only six seasons en route to the trio of titles.

Still, the old nickname lingered. People hadn't forgotten the way that boy from Owensboro, Kentucky, ran off at the mouth. As if they could have.

"I realized when I came into the sport, that it was boring," Waltrip said. "You just had Richard Petty and David Pearson [as major personalities]. We just didn't have any characters.

"And me, I never really agreed with what Richard said or Bobby Allison said or what David said, and I certainly didn't agree with what NASCAR said. They were always protecting themselves and I thought that was a little bit over the top, so I decided I would just be outspoken. But really, it wasn't that I was outspoken. It's just that I spoke. And that was the difference. The other guys were just like, 'yeah, yeah, yeah, yeah,' and I elaborated, in great detail, about the car, the track, whatever happened that day. It was just a different approach.

"I just didn't like a lot of guys and it just didn't really bother me that much."

The feeling was mutual, mainly because Waltrip was winning so much.

Ill will abated. "Jaws," over time, became "DW" and, eventually, "ol' DW" as he evolved into an elder stock car statesman, working for nineteen years as a FOX commentator, retiring in 2019. His trademark line, "Boogity, boogity, boogity," at the start of each race, is now what he is most remembered for by fans.

"You don't like [other drivers] when you're racing with them," Waltrip said. "But once you retire, and they retire, and you kind of see the other side, and then, you kind of get to be friends and you can at least talk about things that have happened.

"The sport needed somebody like me to kind of take it to the next level [of publicity] and I was willing to do that. And I really enjoyed that role for a while . . . but after a while, it's a little bit of a tough row to hoe—nobody likes you and people boo you when you're introduced. That was kind of getting old and in '87 [when I switched to Hendrick Motorsports], I just decided that I had to try and change my image."

That worked too. Waltrip went from driving Johnson's No. 11 Budweiser-sponsored car to a Hendrick Chevrolet sponsored by Tide. The No. 17 Chevrolet—the iconic "Tide Machine"—was part of a new wave of sponsorships aimed at attracting female fans' interest—and loyalty. Waltrip finally won the Daytona 500 in 1989 and imitated Cincinnati Bengals running back Ickey Woods' touchdown celebration, the "Ickey Shuffle." Fans ate that up.

"Jaws" was old news.

"Darrell Waltrip's contributions to the popularity of NASCAR came in two forms: his personality and his talent," said legendary NASCAR journalist Steve Waid. "When he came into NASCAR in 1975, no one—including fans and competitors—had ever seen anything like him. He was brash, cocky, opinionated, and witty. He spoke his mind on everyone and everything. Many fans disliked him because he seemed to show disdain for the stars and veterans who came before him, such as Richard Petty, David Pearson, Bobby Allison, and especially Cale Yarborough. But Waltrip knew what he was doing. By drawing attention to himself—and performing at a high level—he could move up the competitive ranks."

Guess it all worked, ultimately. Waltrip was inducted into the NASCAR Hall of Fame in 2012.

Said DW, "I was blessed in a lot of ways."

(continues on page 125)

(BELOW LEFT) **Junior Johnson (left) and Darrell Waltrip were in the midst of a repeat Cup Series championship season in 1982, proving that two mavericks are almost always better than one when it comes to NASCAR racin'.**

(BELOW RIGHT) **The No. 17 Tide Machine Chevrolet that Waltrip drove to the 1989 Daytona 500 victory.**

DARION CROWDER

THERE ARE BAD RAPS and then there are bad raps. Darion Crowder got one, back on May 4, 1986, at Talladega Superspeedway, when he had the godawful idea to hop in the pace car prior to the start of the Winston 500, then the ninth race of the NASCAR Winston Cup Series season.

It was classic. Law enforcement reacted quickly and hauled the twenty-year-old off to jail, which was a school bus in the infield. One reason this could've happened, right? The guy had to be hammered.

That was incorrect, but the assumption was there. Seemed reasonable, since there were thousands of fans who actually were hammered jammed into NASCAR's biggest track. Whatever, the assumption stuck, the legend grew.

"I would say you have to call him a misunderstood maverick," said Jimmy Creed, former sports editor for the *Anniston* (Alabama) *Star*, who knows the Crowder saga inside and out.

An online search yields too many posts about a drunk guy stealing the Talladega pace car. Thing is, Creed has talked to Talladega County sheriffs who were there, back at the bus. The cops say there was *no indication of intoxication*, a four-word phrase that cops should ask every DUI suspect to repeat, come to think of it.

Here's what there was: a young man who was clearly out of sorts for whatever reason. Crowder's infant son had died two years earlier. His wife had contracted a serious illness; she would die in 1988.

"His life was pretty much falling apart around him," Creed said, citing knowledge gleaned from Talladega's longtime director of public relations, the late Jim Freeman.

The story goes that Crowder wanted to sell his car and start riding a motorcycle to save money. A classified ad about a bike near Talladega looked good. He left his Birmingham home on race morning, drove to Talladega, and took the bike for a quick test ride. Never came back. Crowder rode into the middle of pre-race traffic, then into the track's party-down infield. Eventually, he ditched the bike, hopped a fence, and somehow worked his way into trackside pre-race activity. When the regular pace car driver looked away for a second, Crowder, shirtless, jumped into the bright-red Pontiac Trans Am and hauled ass.

One lap around 2.66-mile Talladega, no problem. By the time the Pontiac made it around to Turn 4 again, though, authorities had his path blocked and he brought the car to a stop. Crowder was yanked from the car, partially by the hair, and hauled away. Fans loved it. Or rather, they loved *Crowder*.

Later that day while in lockup, Crowder got into a fight. That got him transported to Bryce Hospital, a mental health facility in Tuscaloosa. Further indignation: Police got his first name wrong, telling the world it was *Darren*, the way it remains in many accounts today. Maybe it helped a low-profile approach.

Crowder died in 2016. An online obituary has only his Alabama driver's license photo. Thirty years after Talladega, one photo online?

"I have not been able to find anything else out about the guy," Creed said in 2023.

Neither have we. The speedway staff tried too a few years back. There was talk about inviting Crowder back for a legitimate pace car ride. They might've even let him drive again. Can you imagine? A hillbilly hero's return. But they couldn't find him.

Not even the local sheriff's office could help. A records department employee said the arrest record for Crowder "had been lost."

Said Creed, "It's like he fell off the face of the map."

Sad story.

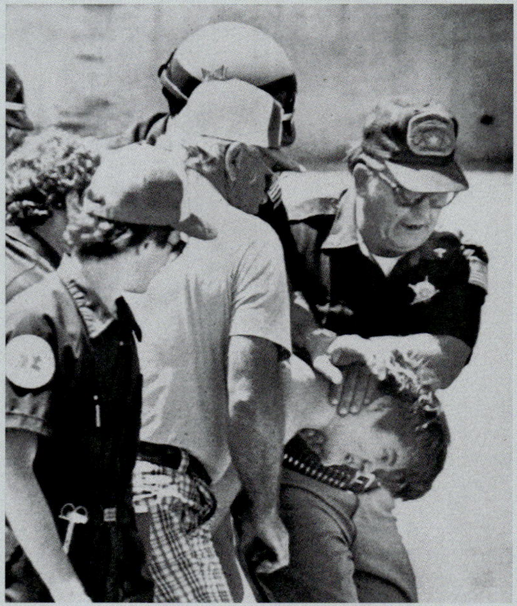

Darion Crowder is being treated harshly by law enforcement in this May 4, 1988, photo, but context is needed: the car he's being pulled from is the pace car for the Winston 500 being held that day at Talladega Superspeedway. Crowder had just parked the Pontiac after commandeering (stealing) it for a couple joy-riding laps around the 2.66-mile track. The cops were not in a good mood to say the least.

HUMPY WHEELER

FOR ALL THE BIG personalities, all the fantastic photographic finishes, for all the legendary venues on the racing calendar—all the storylines and hype that make NASCAR such a popular sport—there's plenty of good argument that one of the sport's greatest showmen never even raced in NASCAR himself.

Instead, Humpy Wheeler made his name making others' names, and for decades creating a level of excitement at the track for NASCAR fans never before seen and never equaled.

Although Wheeler worked for decades as a track president, eventually overseeing one of NASCAR's most preeminent properties, Charlotte Motor Speedway, for thirty-three years, his passion as one of the sport's great promoters will always be the part of his résumé remembered most.

Wheeler was widely considered the "P. T. Barnum" of NASCAR, a frequent and valid comparison to the great circus founder. His ideas and work drew fans to the racetrack for a full-sensory, always-thrilling, "ultimate" experience—and so frequently won over new eyeballs for the sport in the process.

A double-degree college graduate, Wheeler's formal education in journalism and political science served him well. His understanding of "the sell" distinguished him from colleagues and was a massive boost to Charlotte Motor Speedway at a time when the sport was just beginning to flourish.

His pre-race shows were legendary. From a taxi race to a reenactment of the military invasion of Grenada . . . he brought in elephants for an impromptu circus, loved a thrilling school bus jump, and even managed an emotionally moving Guinness Book of World Records mark, gathering more than five thousand firemen at the Charlotte track shortly after the September 11, 2001, attacks.

Legendary actress Elizabeth Taylor even served as a Grand Marshal.

Nothing seemed off the table when it came to celebrating Charlotte Motor Speedway and the sport of NASCAR. If Wheeler could envision it, he was ready to make it happen.

"I always thought the nickname 'Humpy' didn't do justice to Humpy Wheeler because, while it brought him the attention he craved, the goofy nickname tended to minimize his keen intellect," author and longtime motorsports reporter Bob Zeller said.

"He was a great interview because he always had a perspective on the sport or the current happenings that was different than the usual take. . . . Humpy could converse on just about any subject. He was completely comfortable in the media center milling around with the writers, perhaps because he spent a short time as a newspaper reporter himself."

The hard work and great imagination Wheeler put in was respected, especially as NASCAR was growing from a regionally beloved sport into a bona fide national pastime. Wheeler's work was a sort of art form, perhaps not fully appreciated at the time for the serious positive ramifications it had for the sport he loved.

"He didn't earn the nickname of Barnum and Bailey for nothing," former NASCAR President Mike Helton told the *Sports Business Journal*. "We had a lot of characters pioneering track development, but as the sport started to explode, Humpy took it to a new level. Other track promoters would look at him and say, 'I wish I had the moxie to do that.'"

Moxie was never a problem for Wheeler, who despite the sometimes outlandish publicity stunts, actually went about business with a keen knowledge of "the sell." Having started his career in a time when NASCAR was still competing for the Sunday national fandom, he understood being "bold" was a favorable distinction.

Wheeler walked that fine line between publicity stunt and gravitational pull that put people in the grandstands and sold the sport nationally. His vision and ability to turn a "Why not?" into a "Hell yeah!" made him an essential difference maker in the sport and that legacy remains an important contribution that will be felt far into perpetuity.

Firestone tire representative Humpy Wheeler discusses, presumably, treadwear, with Goodyear's Crash Grant.

RESTRICTOR PLATE RACING

LOVE IT OR HATE IT, restrictor plate racing had to happen in 1988.

In the May 1987 Winston 500 at 2.66-mile Talladega Superspeedway, Allison's Buick got sideways and flew airborne into the catch fence along Talladega's front straightaway. For a couple of terrifying moments, the car appeared headed into the grandstands—and unspeakable tragedy. The fence, although more than 100 feet of it was sheared away when the car impacted, did its job, holding—and flinging—the Buick back down to asphalt earth.

Only three spectators required medical treatment for—given the potential—relatively minor injuries. NASCAR had been only another moment away from the worst motorsports accident since the 1955 24 Hours of Le Mans, when debris flew into a tightly packed trackside crowd, killing eighty-three spectators and injuring more than one hundred. If his car had gone completely through the fence, the numbers would've dwarfed those at Le Mans. No telling what the aftermath might have been but government intervention, sponsor reaction, and ultimately a shutdown come to mind as possibilities. (Allison, in true "Alabama Gang" fashion, walked away from the carnage.)

Another tilt of the good ol' axis. NASCAR reacted three days later by mandating that smaller carburetors would be used at both Talladega and its "sister" track, 2.5-mile Daytona International Speedway, resulting in significantly reduced speeds. That took care of the remaining 1987 races on the Cup Series' two biggest tracks. When the '88 season came back around, NASCAR went further with a new mandate: carburetor restrictor plates at Daytona and 'Dega to seriously restrict air flow to the engine. Horsepower plummeted from 650 to the 400 range. The era of nose-to-tail pack racing on the high banks had arrived and with it, a whole separate set of safety concerns.

NASCAR occasionally restricting speeds was nothing new (from 1971 to '74, plates were used on specified big-block engines), but this was different. So was Allison's crash.

Daytona and Talladega were different animals—then and now. They bite.

Oh, there has been controversy aplenty since the advent of the plates, which have evolved in the fuel-injection era to a "tapered spacer" that also limits air flow. For years, it was drivers and fans saying NASCAR should let 'em rip at the two tri-ovals . . . restrictors be damned! Dale Earnhardt himself said restrictor plate racing had reduced the glamour of the Daytona 500.

Glamour be damned! Without plates, speeds would have continued to climb and, before long, stock cars would've resembled 727s, with Turn 4 the main runway. NASCAR had proof, sort of, in 2004 when Rusty Wallace tested a car at Talladega without a plate. Top speed: 228 mph. *Flight attendants, prepare the cabin for takeoff.*

Wallace called the idea of racing sans plates insane, especially with pack racing.

Folks, this had to happen. If you don't agree, go read about Le Mans 1955 and get back to us.

(ABOVE) **In 1988, NASCAR changed from the 1987 "quick-fix"— smaller carburetors—to carburetor restrictor plates for races at Daytona International Speedway and Talladega Superspeedway. Plates reduced the air and fuel flow—and horsepower. The era of "pack racing" on the high banks had come to NASCAR, for better or worse, in the name of safety.**

(OPPOSITE) **In the May 1987 Winston 500, Bobby Allison's car took flight during a front stretch crash at Talladega. The car nearly cleared the catch fence and went into the grandstands. An unthinkable tragedy averted, NASCAR mandated smaller carburetors for the next two races at NASCAR's biggest tracks, Talladega and Daytona, to slow speeds.**

22
Winston Cup

OFFICIAL FUEL
76
DU PONT
GMAC
MOOG
CLEVITE
Prestone
SIMPSON
Edelbrock
plasti-kote
TE CARLO
24

CHAPTER 6

THE 1990s

BILL JR., BRUTON, AND "THE HAT MAN"

One item that helped define this decade was the youth movement that started when a young California driver, Jeff Gordon, came on board and almost immediately began winning races. In a sport that featured drivers in their mid- to late thirties, the age was dropping each year, with many drivers coming from the open wheel ranks. As the older drivers retired, there seemed to be another crop of youngsters to take their place. And the kids were good race drivers. Several went on to win NASCAR championships.

NASCAR FINALLY CAME to the Indianapolis Motor Speedway after years of speculation. It was always a dream of "Big Bill" France to bring his boys to the Brickyard. In fact, France was on the winning team of the 1946 Indy 500 and as early as 1948 it was mentioned in print about how exciting it would be to run the stock cars there. NASCAR tested at Indy in 1993 with the first "Brickyard 400" being run in 1994. And, as you might have guessed, the youngster Jeff Gordon won that inaugural event.

New speedways in Ft. Worth, Texas, Las Vegas, Nevada, Nashville, Tennessee, and Kansas City, Kansas, opened the opportunity to bring NASCAR to more top markets. The International Speedway Corporation bought the interests in several speedways from Roger Penske, gaining tracks in California, Arizona, and Michigan, and also acquired ownership to Martinsville from the Earles family. Bruton Smith founded Speedway Motorsports, which was based in Charlotte. His interests included Bristol, Charlotte, and later New Hampshire and Atlanta Motor Speedways and the road course at Sonoma.

(PREVIOUS) **Jeff Gordon pits his DuPont Chevrolet during the 1999 Pennzoil 400 at Homestead-Miami Speedway. He finished tenth and went on to end up sixth in the series championship won by Bobby Labonte. Gordon was in his prime at the time, having won championships in 1995, '97 and '98. He added his fourth and final title in 2001.**

BILL FRANCE JR.

William Clifton France, chances are you know him as Bill France Jr., was a certain maverick but also a calculated one. Following the inimitable lead of his father, NASCAR founder and first president William Henry Getty France—"Big Bill"—Bill Jr. took over as NASCAR president in 1971. Never looked back.

He advanced NASCAR far beyond even his father's vast vision, with a corporate leadership style undeniably all his own, not even close to today's politically correct standards, tough love to the max for employees but still somewhat beloved by many, if not most, of the people who worked for him until his 2007 death.

Under Bill Jr., NASCAR's autocracy really had evolved, albeit leading to the well-worn phrase soon attached to the son: *benevolent dictatorship*. He could and would welcome dissent on topics, in the office and at the racetrack. That never meant he was ever going to agree. Surprise.

He was an unforgettable man, one of those characters who walked, and talked, a lot taller than he actually strode or stood. He had a presence, fueled by an unending verbal library of adages, sayings, and slogans to emphasize whatever point he was either trying to make, or trying to bury. Most of the library was of his own making; the rest, he made his own.

Meetings were a prime stage. One wrong turn might lead to a missive.

One of the most memorable: Bill Jr. emphasizing the importance of teamwork. "We all have to be pissing through the same straw." If any reader has ever witnessed the pissing through the straw phenomenon, well, good for you. Still, Bill made his point.

Bill France Jr. replaced his father as NASCAR president in 1972. He, in turn, was replaced as NASCAR chairman and CEO by his son Brian France in 2003. Bill Jr. led NASCAR during an era of unprecedented growth with a management style all his own.

Bill Jr. was hands on when it came to learning the business of NASCAR. This picture is evidence of that, as it shows the future NASCAR boss driving a grader on what looks like the future backstretch.

The date was January 10, 1972. The photo was staged but the implications were as real as possible. Bill France Sr., NASCAR's founder and first president, was handing over the reins—and the office keys (it looks like)—to his son Bill France Jr.

These words of wisdom lasted. Former NASCAR Vice President Paul Brooks, who worked closely with Bill Jr., collected them. He called them "Billisms." He has shared them and that is a good thing. It's maverick worthy, without a doubt. Some classic Billisms follow. Brief explanations provided as considered needed. Not everyone knows this stuff.

"You may be trying to put a saddle on a cow." Bill Jr.'s view on what he considered an overambitious project. That had to sting.

"Now, you're just a stringer, right?" A less-than-cordial greeting for a reporter from a major newspaper, highlighting their free-lance status, before a key interview. Nothing like setting the tone.

"This is hurting me more than it's helping you." Uttered during a meeting going down the tubes.

"You are talking out of both sides of your mouth . . . and your ass." Bill Jr. talking to a nervous employee.

"He pulls his gun out and puts five bullets in his foot before he gets his gun in the air." His view on a business associate who was fast, loose, and sloppy.

"A lunch with Hunter will be better than a last supper with me." Bill Jr.'s instructions for feuding coworkers to seek counsel from NASCAR Vice President Jim Hunter, unless they wanted to get real.

"This is a movie, not a snapshot." Bill Jr.'s way of describing a long-term business approach.

"He pulled his gun out after we had checked ours at the door." Bill Jr.'s description of a meeting gone south, after the negotiations turned "hard ball." Another gun reference. Told you Bill Jr. was a maverick.

THE WORD "DEAL." It was the backbone of NASCAR lexicon at the sport's outset. Bill Jr. took to the word like few in the sport, perhaps second only to Richard Petty. "It was one of them racing deals."

Some deal-infused Billisms:

"Ever since Judas did the deal with the thirty pieces of silver, there has been a price for anything." Self-explanatory and a good one.

"I couldn't get the pencil to work on that deal." Turning down a bad proposition.

"You can't find the end of the string on that deal." Bill Jr. knew a financial pit when he saw one.

"Everybody's still here working? Good deal." The day before Thanksgiving, acknowledging employees on the way out the door of NASCAR's offices.

EMPLOYEES WORKING HARD. Long hours. No clock punching in NASCAR. Bill France Jr. embodied those notions, and he loved to one-up employees when it came to perceived commitment to the job.

One morning, several NASCAR executives boarded a company jet bound for Charlotte. As the plane taxied down the runway, then-Chief Operating Officer George Pyne brought up a current hot topic, wondering what the media were saying about it that morning. It was early. Not everyone was properly informed. Guess who was?

"Here, Pyne," Bill Jr. said gruffly, reaching into his briefcase, flinging thirty or so pages, fresh off the printer, onto Pyne's lap. "Read the clips." The old man had done his own internet research, not long after dawn, in his office.

Brooks has a good one.

"I would always make sure I was in the office every day before Bill arrived," Brooks said. "Bill and I had been following an important legal case that involved another sports league and for weeks I would keep him posted on what was happening. One morning, I had a real meeting outside of the office. When I returned, Bill had left his business card on my desk with a note written on the back that said *'8:40 a.m. . . . Paul, you must have overslept. Anyway, the league lost their suit. Have a nice day. —Bill'*

"I was crushed that Bill beat me to the office that day. He knew leaving this note would get under my skin and he was eager to share this news with me first, before I had heard . . . and he gave me a little jab along the way! To this day, I keep his business card on my desk as a nice reminder of Bill, his wisdom, his prodding, and to remember to stay on top of the business issues at hand."

Bill France Jr. battled health issues throughout the last decade of his life. He left us with some Billisms on the way out.

"The last time I tried to walk on water I fell right through to the bottom." Talking in 2000 about his medical treatments.

"How am I doing? Well, I'm on the right side of the grass and there are no roots growing out of my ass." –A regular Billism, in the later years of his life.

"The calendar got him." His reaction to an associate's death.

The calendar got Bill France Jr. on June 4, 2007. One of those deals.

O. BRUTON SMITH

BRUTON SMITH is in the NASCAR Hall of Fame, which some consider an upset akin to Derrike Cope winning the Daytona 500. After all, Smith spent a large part of his large life at odds with various members of the France family.

This goes way back. We're talking the late 1940s when NASCAR founder Bill France Sr. was trying to get his idea of a Strictly Stock Division to fly. It was struggling, in part because the Charlotte-based National Stock Car Racing Association (NSCRA) was holding races for the same type of showroom-to-racetrack sedans that France considered the future of American motorsports. Or at least, of NASCAR.

And guess who headed NSCRA? Bruton Smith. That is, until he was drafted into the Korean War in 1951. It is not a stretch to say that Smith's military service likely helped NASCAR. Weird, right? But Smith was already a helluva promoter, and he had no qualms about facing down "Big Bill" France, even though, technically, he would've needed a stepladder to do that. There were reports of a possible "merger" of the two organizations. The real world intervened.

Smith got drafted in January. The NSCRA folded that summer.

LET'S MOVE ON, to 1960. Smith and driver Curtis Turner had combined resources to build Charlotte Motor Speedway. Financial constraints had led Turner to seek a loan from the Teamsters Union, which in turn wanted Turner to help organize a union. Bill France Sr. squashed the union idea and banned Turner from NASCAR. Sort of guilt by association this time around for Bruton, but still.

Legal problems got Smith booted from the speedway's board in 1962. He started another business: selling cars. Made a ton of money, a decent amount spent on shares of Charlotte Motor Speedway stock. He was coming back, to the house that he built, by God. Overheard in the halls of NASCAR's offices: "Shit."

Bill France Jr. inherited the Bruton Smith relationship when he replaced his father as NASCAR president in 1972. And with that came a new dynamic a decade later: Smith's complete takeover of Charlotte Motor Speedway in 1985 and the founding of Speedway Motorsports Incorporated (SMI) in 1994.

That put SMI into indirect competition with the International Speedway Corporation (ISC), the company that, like SMI, owned racetracks that hosted NASCAR Cup Series events. The indirect turned pretty goddamn direct sometimes when it came to race dates, and that led to a 2004 lawsuit filed against NASCAR and ISC by an SMI shareholder. Gotta ask: Is that enough acronyms for you?

The suit was settled and awarded SMI's Texas Motor Speedway a second NASCAR Sprint Cup race. Groundbreaking. Bruton popped Champagne. We can't confirm, but you know he did.

Eddie Gossage, who worked for Smith both as Charlotte Motor Speedway public relations director and Texas Motor Speedway president, said Smith's disputes with the Frances demand perspective.

"I don't think he really relished it," Gossage said, "but he did want them to know that they didn't build the sport alone, and that it needed to be fairer. He would point to things he did, and he could name a long list of others that did things."

The decades-long cloud hanging over the Smith-France families has lifted in recent years. Both Bill France Sr. and Bill Jr. are gone, as is Bruton Smith. Both organizations have new leadership—Bill Jr.'s brother Jim France for NASCAR, Bruton's son, Marcus, for SMI. Also need to remember that the thawing out started while Brian France was NASCAR's chairman and CEO.

"My dad and Brian had a pretty good relationship," Marcus Smith said. "He wanted to help Brian. My dad always had a passion to try to help the sport and to grow the sport.

"We've all gotta work together. And I think that there's a lot of [ongoing] collaboration that's really important for the whole sport."

Bruton Smith died in 2022 at the age of ninety-five, six years after his NASCAR Hall of Fame induction that was well-deserved for a body of work that included running a sanctioning body, promoting races, building speedways, building the business of SMI—and, occasionally, jousting with Bill France Sr. and Bill Jr.

Smith's acceptance speech at the induction ceremony was neither confrontational nor conciliatory. But it still had a "bygones" feel.

"I want to thank all the people who voted for me," Smith said. "That was wonderful. You took a chance."

Not really. After all these years, it's clear. There was no upset here.

"It's amazing . . . what's really cool is that my dad, he dealt with Bill France Sr., with Bill France Jr., with Brian France, with Jim France," Marcus said. "And he was *there* at the beginning of it all, before NASCAR was NASCAR."

(continues on page 138)

O. Bruton Smith built Speedway Motorsports Incorporated, a parallel stock car universe adjacent to the International Speedway Corporation, NASCAR's longtime "sister" company. Building SMI meant building some of the finest oval tracks in the world.

Bruton Smith was around for the early days of NASCAR and tried to establish an alternative stock car circuit at one point. He had the chops, having started promoting races at the age of seventeen. He's pictured here with another of the sport's true mavericks, driver Fonty Flock.

TOM HIGGINS AND STEVE WAID

THEY WERE INSEPARABLE at the racetrack. In the garage area, people called them "a corporation." They were only partly joking.

Tom Higgins and Steve Waid were accomplished sports journalists back when that really meant something. Back when you held the news in your hands each day and all other sources were complements. You know, exactly the opposite of today's landscape.

Higgins and Waid sure meant something to NASCAR fans for more than thirty years, with coverage that came from the inside but was written for every reader.

Higgins' sports writing career took him from the *Canton* (North Carolina) *Enterprise*, the *Asheville* (North Carolina) *Times* and, finally, the *Charlotte Observer* in 1964. In 1980, he became the first NASCAR beat writer in the country to cover a full NASCAR season.

Waid first covered NASCAR for the *Martinsville* (Virginia) *Bulletin* before establishing himself at the *Roanoke* (Virginia) *Times*. Feeling his established oats, Waid took a chance that came in big, going to *Grand National Scene*, basically the NASCAR Bible, delivered from the stock car heavens once a week. The magazine changed names twice, from *Winston Cup Scene*, then *NASCAR Scene*. Waid advanced to publisher.

Now that we got that stuff out of the way, the Higgins-Waid combination—or was it Waid-Higgins? Who cares? They didn't.

"We never took ourselves seriously," Waid said.

However the combo may have been worded, it worked, on and off the track. These boys were a story-breaking machine and traveling comedy duo, following the work hard, play hard NASCAR battle call. They were like Hawkeye and Trapper from the old TV show *M*A*S*H*. They were celebrities. They had their own NASCAR trading cards. Every media center belonged to them, and every race weekend was worth celebrating. And we do mean celebrating.

"We never missed a party, that's for sure, and everybody knew it," Waid said, "but by the same token, we never missed a deadline. We were able to make some pretty good hay."

They didn't miss many stories, these two, partly because they literally were a combination at the track, their working relationship blurring journalism ethics a bit. Maybe more than a bit. They shared leads, and scoops. That's how they got to know each other. Waid, a young pup at *Roanoke*, was covering a race and a big story broke. Higgins missed most of the day due to a serious family commitment. When he finally arrived at the media center, Waid introduced himself by filling Higgins in on the news. The *Observer* had the story, the next morning. Waid had a friend, for life.

Roanoke and *Charlotte* weren't competing against each other. Likewise, *Scene*, being a weekly, was never in direct competition with the *Observer*, or vice versa. At least that's the way Higgins and Waid saw it in those pre-internet days. Aside from stories, they also shared their talents. And then there's the fact that Higgins freelanced for *Scene*. Maybe that makes all of this moot. The takeaway is that these guys had a helluva thing going, to the benefit of readers.

They found time to co-author a fine book. *Junior Johnson: Brave in Life* made perfect sense. The old moonshiners, telling these two characters his story. Where are the tapes?

So there really was something to that corporation stuff. There definitely was something to the relationship stuff.

Said Waid, "Everybody knew we breathed through the same lungs. Everybody knew we were best friends."

Higgins, called "Pappy" by so many of his friends, received NASCAR's Squier-Hall Award for Media Excellence in 2015. He died in 2017, days short of his eighty-first birthday.

"I'm supposed to have a command of words, but the only word I can come up with is 'flabbergasted,'" Higgins said on the day of his award announcement. "To dream that I would ever achieve anything like this . . . it's just beyond my wildest expectations."

And so, of course, Waid completed the corporation sweep, receiving the Squier-Hall Award in 2019.

"It's nice to have your work recognized, that you did something that somebody recognized and appreciated," Waid said after receiving his award. "That means more than anything else."

(LEFT) **Tom Higgins, a fine journalist and a finer man, helped define NASCAR media coverage as the sport grew exponentially in the 1980s and '90s. He also had one helluva good time doing so.**

(BELOW) **Tom Higgins and Steve Waid were journalists first--and characters throughout their careers. They became part of the NASCAR Cup Series landscape. Never missed a party. Never missed a deadline. So, of course, they had their own trading card.**

In a race some consider NASCAR's greatest, Alan Kulwicki edged several rivals to win the NASCAR Cup Series championship. His final points margin was a mere ten over Bill Elliott—then the closest points finish in Series history.

ALAN KULWICKI

IT WAS TIME. In the early 1990s, NASCAR was undergoing another important transition from race teams who essentially succeeded by the seat of their pants to a garage full of competitors who began seeking—and benefitting from—a more formal education.

Alan Kulwicki's 1992 NASCAR Cup Series championship was a conglomeration of these two forces in the NASCAR garage, but his title and the self-guided drive that earned him the sport's biggest trophy is something appreciated even decades later. It was absolutely transformational.

The proud Wisconsin native owned, drove, and served as his own chief engineer on his No. 7 Ford that eventually earned that 1992 NASCAR title—a passion project like no other NASCAR had seen at the elite level. For so many decades there had been mechanics who tuned these stock cars to dominant season outputs. And there were drivers whose skill behind the wheel could produce even odds against victory.

But until Kulwicki's sport-changing championship run, formal education and true engineering prowess were hardly résumé showstoppers on the stock car scene. For so many decades, NASCAR's brand of racing had instead advanced thanks more to the hard work, instinctual care, and a whole lot of flying by the seat of the pants.

And then came Kulwicki, from parts unfamiliar, speaking a new technical language and bringing previously undefined expectations and operating procedures with him. It took Kulwicki only a handful of years to turn his 1986 NASCAR Cup Series Rookie of the Year Award—with only a single car and two engines for the season—into the biggest championship in his sport. And he did it his way, a distinguishing feature for a driver who openly chose and embraced going about things differently.

Kulwicki was, indeed, a trailblazer and maverick.

Much of that was the unique approach he brought to NASCAR. For starters, Kulwicki understood the physics of a race car thanks to a mechanical engineering degree he earned when many who crowded the garage—let alone fellow drivers—never even seriously considered going to college in that era of NASCAR competition.

It was quickly apparent that Kulwicki was more interested in the science and competition—and winning—than simply making best friends with others in the garage. He was very studious and often described as a loner. But truly, it was just a different approach to the same big goal he shared with his competition: winning races and championships.

The final six-race run to the 1992 NASCAR Cup Series title was as intense as many remember, and this was more than a decade before NASCAR revamped its championship format to include an elimination-style title run.

Huge fan favorites Davey Allison and Bill Elliott joined Kulwicki as the group of final contenders with varying results in the races leading up to the championship finale at Atlanta Motor Speedway.

While all three drivers led laps in the championship race, Allison's title hopes were eliminated in an early accident. And although Elliott won the race and led Kulwicki across the finish line, Kulwicki had amassed a ten-point advantage—thanks to a strategy that included leading the most laps in the race—over the popular Georgia native to ultimately claim the NASCAR Cup Series title.

Kulwicki was the first driver not to hail from the Southeast portion of the country to earn the series trophy, the first champion driver with a four-year college degree, and it all came in the closest championship finish in the sport's modern history.

Fittingly, Kulwicki celebrated his championship with the Polish victory lap—a celebratory lap in reverse around the speedway, still done today in his honor. Proud of his Polish roots, Kulwicki explained that by driving to the right around the oval, he was closer to the fans and could wave to them; something very important to him. And to the fans, who appreciated his exceptional, if unorthodox, championship path.

Veteran motorsports reporter and author Bob Zeller covered Kulwicki's career and remembers well Kulwicki's passionate drive, a self-made run against the established well-funded teams and the unique approach Kulwicki took into the championship.

"He [Kulwicki] said in the heat of the championship run he had actually studied how to be a champion, and had read Vince Lombardi's book *What It Takes to Be #1*, to adopt the mental attitude he felt he needed to triumph in the ultracompetitive Cup Series," Zeller recalled.

Tragically, Kulwicki, thirty-eight, was killed in a plane crash outside Bristol, Tennessee, only five months after celebrating his sport-changing championship. His five career NASCAR Cup Series race victories hardly reflective of the massive impact Alan Kulwicki had on his sport—unprecedented advancements and expectations benefitting NASCAR racing to this day.

(continues on page 142)

The car was called the "Underbird" because of its presumed underdog status, which turned out to be an illusion. Owner-driver Alan Kulwicki won the 1992 NASCAR Cup Series championship.

BILL BRODRICK

FOR MORE THAN twenty-nine years, Bill Brodrick created, then assumed, then thrived in a high-profile alter ego—"The Hat Man."

Chances are you remember him. The big, red-haired, bearded man from UNOCAL, so visible in NASCAR Cup Series Victory Lane ceremonies from 1969 through '97. The guy was as known to fans as Pearson, Petty, Darrell, or Dale, with his swept-back hair, aviator shades, and eight or so rings, rapidly switching out different hats for winners' sponsorships photos.

Hat Man.

Brodrick, all he did was, basically, create today's NASCAR Victory Lane ceremony that honors everyone except the doctor who delivered the winning driver.

The '69 Daytona 500 was his first race with UNOCAL. "Victory Lane was a wild, chaotic zoo back then," Brodrick recalled in 2023.

"The photographers couldn't get pictures, TV people were screaming and hollering, and it was just total confusion. I wanted to look out for the company, so after a race or two, I said, 'Hey, wait a minute, let's just hold on everybody. Let's just take it easy and we'll give everybody a chance to get what they need. Photographers can get their pictures, TV can get their interviews, radio can do their thing at the start. If anybody needs to make any presentations, we'll do that, and the sponsors can do their stuff.'

"And you know, we just kind of took over out of necessity in order for Union 76 to get the publicity we wanted from Victory Lane. Because nobody was getting anything."

(ABOVE) **When Bobby Allison won the 1982 Daytona 500, Ned Jarrett of CBS was in Victory Lane to interview the new champion—and UNOCAL's Bill Brodrick was right in the middle of it all.**

(LEFT) **Ah, Brodrick in the early years, 1971 to be exact, greeting Firecracker 400 winner Bobby Isaac postrace at Daytona International Speedway.**

Bill Brodrick became known as "The Hat Man" as he revamped NASCAR Cup Series Victory Lane activities for nearly three decades, in the process becoming a true NASCAR personality himself.

Brodrick said nobody complained. The sense of order had to be welcomed. Before long, it became clear that Victory Lane belonged to UNOCAL and the 6 foot 3 inch (1 m 86 cm) Hat Man, now the zookeeper. Or rather, gatekeeper. Brodrick determined who entered his realm, and then he controlled the flow of proceedings. It was still frenzied in there, but with newfound purpose. Interviews proceeded. Trophies were presented. And hats were worn, then changed, repeatedly, for various promotional shots.

For nearly three decades, NASCAR had a rock star in Brodrick. It stayed that way until 1997, when Brodrick parted ways with Tosco, the company that had bought UNOCAL.

"In time, and almost certainly because of his compelling appearance, Brodrick grew to become a racing institution," wrote Al Pearce, co-author of NASCAR 75 Years, in the Rocky Mount Telegram. "He signed autographs, had his own trading card, registered 'The Hat Man' as a personal trademark, and was as easily recognized in public as any driver in the world."

"When we were there, it was fun," Brodrick said. At the age of eighty-five, he sounded like he could still run a good post-race scene.

"We had a good time and the best part of it all was being there to make sure that the guy who won the race got what he deserved. His pictures with his family, with his girlfriend, with his minister, with whoever. Everybody would go out of Victory Lane happy and that was the bottom line."

RAY EVERNHAM AND THE RAINBOW WARRIORS

EVERNHAM IS OUR MAVERICK, but a guy named Andy Papathanassiou is the grand facilitator in this tale. Together, they changed the way pit crews were assembled and, in the process, they changed NASCAR.

Evernham, a former modified driver, already was developing a rep as an innovator, but this was different, an out-of-the-box move, the 1992 hiring of Papathanassiou—who came to be called Papa for obvious reasons. Papa became the first pit crew coach in NASCAR history for what would become one of the most famous pit crews in NASCAR history—the brand-new Rainbow Warriors, the guys with the bright uniforms, getting hotshot Wonder Boy Jeff Gordon and the No. 24 DuPont Chevrolet on and off pit road.

Previously, pit crews in the NASCAR Cup Series ranged from the Wood Brothers' consistently choreographed excellence to a range of efficiencies—or inefficiencies, as it were. Back in the 1960s, Ford suggested to Leonard Wood the possibility of cutting time spent in the pits. Leonard proceeded to lead a revamping of the typical NASCAR stop, shaving valuable seconds off routine stops especially, seconds that added up and played a big role in the Woods' success.

Evernham's approach, which ultimately paid off with three Cup Series championships and forty-seven victories as Gordon's crew chief, was the same at its core: Find new ways to do things quicker, without losing efficiency. Evernham's inherent short track sensibility—he had slung some tires himself through the years—led him to start with the people doing the work. And that's where we're talking next-level action.

"When we started this team, the whole time we were building race cars and a shop, we were [also] building a pit crew," Evernham told the *Boston Globe* that year.

Papathanassiou, a former Stanford football player, had worked on Alan Kulwicki's 1992 championship team as a tire changer before coming to Hendrick Motorsports.

The new partnership ushered in the age of athletes onto NASCAR's pit road. Other former football players and guys who played other sports followed Papa's lead. This got serious, everyone chasing the rainbow.

(LEFT) **The Rainbow Warriors in action were a sight to behold, with pit stop times that had you re-checking your stopwatch. This was pre-digital, remember.**

(OPPOSITE) **Ray Evernham altered the NASCAR landscape in the late 1990s by hiring top-notch athletes from other sports to form the legendary "Rainbow Warriors" pit crew that helped Jeff Gordon win four championships.**

Evernham downplays the notion he started a revolution, saying, "Really it was just evolution. There were a lot of guys thinking about it and starting to dabble with it.

"We were fortunate enough to have started with a clean sheet of paper when I went to Hendrick Motorsports. Rick is quite a visionary and he just told me, 'Look, you build this team however you want.' He really put me in charge. Honestly, from watching all the films and watching the races and watching that stuff, I knew there was a lot of time to be gained on pit road. I just [expanded upon] what the Wood Brothers had done [years earlier]."

"Pit crews are sort of like a football team," Papa told the *Tampa Tribune* in 2000. "We treat crew members like the athletes they are, and train them like athletes."

Athletes are everywhere, on every pit road, these days. Evernham's handiwork.

Evernham was inducted into the NASCAR Hall of Fame in 2018. As of 2024, only six crew chiefs were in the Hall: Evernham, Dale Inman, Leonard Wood, Kirk Shelmerdine, Waddell Wilson, and Chad Knaus.

"The Rainbow Warriors were the greatest ever," Evernham said at his induction. "I loved leading that team. They were a real team, built on trust, honesty, and respect."

After the Warriors, Evernham went after new challenges, starting with leading Dodge's return to NASCAR, with his own team. In this decade, he started the SRX Series, and has secured the rights to the IROC brand, plotting a comeback, no doubt.

T-REX

THIS TALE WAS short, sweet, and dynamic. In 1997, Hendrick Motorsports brought a most unique car to compete in NASCAR's annual All-Star Race, then known as The Winston, at Charlotte Motor Speedway that paid a total purse of $1,000,000. They called the car "T-Rex" due to sponsorship from the new *Jurassic Park* movie and the dinosaur on the hood. This was apt. The car was a beast.

It also was illegal.

One and done, that was this deal for that No. 24 Chevrolet driven by Jeff Gordon. Gordon's innovative crew chief Ray Evernham has a classic memory of being called into the NASCAR hauler after that race. NASCAR President Bill France Jr. wanted to visit. Bill let Ray know that while the car may have passed inspection that night, it wouldn't in the future.

What was sketchy about T-Rex?

"Pretty much everything," recalled Gary Nelson, then the Winston Cup Series director. "There was no major single item you could point to and say, 'You'll be okay if you fix that.' Yeah, it was pretty much everything."

And because of that race, T-Rex became even more ominous. Downright threatening to the sport. Implications went far beyond that evening's cool million.

"The biggest thing was that if we had let that car race in the future," Nelson said, "it would've immediately obsoleted all of the other cars in the series."

Evernham experimented primarily with things like springs and the car's sway bar. He had something special, as pre-race testing had shown. And then there was the Gordon factor. The 1995 series champion was amid his second championship season. A weekly favorite no matter the car.

Gordon's dominance blew T-Rex's cover.

"If it wasn't for Jeff Gordon driving that car, it might still be legal," Evernham said in 2018. "And now there's all this legend that we had 'super this' and 'super that' on it but it was just a really well-built race car . . . Jeff Gordon decided to put his foot to the floor at the height of his career and just smoked those guys. He was running laps seven- and eight-tenths faster than the rest of the field."

Said Gordon, "I put the hammer down and everything worked out our way."

(OPPOSITE) **The ultimate one-and-done in terms of NASCAR: T-Rex, the tricked-out Chevrolet that went carnivore, devouring the competition at the 1997 NASCAR All-Star Race, then called "The Winston." After Jeff Gordon's victory, NASCAR Chairman and CEO Bill France Jr. informed his team that the car would be illegal moving forward.**

24
DUPONT
AUTOMOTIVE FINISHES
1-800-MARROW-2
PEPSI
Frosted Mini-Wheats
GMAC
MONTE CARLO
GOODYEAR
Western Auto
MOOG
plasti-kote
SIMPSON
Edelbrock
True Value
MCI
BUSCH
SPICER
CLEVITE
RCA
3M
Holley
Bowman
JESEL

20
GOODYEAR
mbna
3M
MOOG
CLEVITE
COMP
WIX
Edelbrock
EAGLE

CHAPTER 7

THE 2000s

BRIAN, THE BUSCH BROTHERS, AND TONY STEWART—MAVERICKS EVERYWHERE

A dark episode for the sport occurred when Dale Earnhardt lost his life at Daytona in 2001. But the sport endured and fans found a new hero in his son, Dale Jr. Many safety features, which were in the works at the time, were expedited into the sport. SAFER Barriers, or soft walls, the HANS device, and wraparound seats have offered immense safety to the drivers since. There have been no deaths in more than two decades.

A NEW CHAPTER in NASCAR occurred when its long-time president Bill France, Jr. retired, handing the reigns to his son, Brian, who brought wide, sweeping changes to the sport. He instituted the playoff point system and brought new major sponsors into the sport, which included the TV package, the official fuel, and the title sponsor for the Cup Series.

The youth movement continued as the brash Busch brothers came from Las Vegas, with Kyle Busch making his first NASCAR Craftsman Truck Series start at sixteen years old. After that, NASCAR instituted a rule that no driver could start a major series event until they were eighteen. Today, drivers in their late teens making it to the big time is common.

A new "Car of Tomorrow," or "Gen 6" as it was called, made its debut. The car was designed with safety in mind. The roof was raised a few inches to provide larger window openings in case the driver had to be extricated. The driver's seat was moved several inches inward toward the center of the car and high-impact foam was installed in the driver's door. A large wing was installed on the rear of the car and a special front air dam, or valance, was added to the front of the car for added stability. This new design gave mavericks less opportunities to ply their craft.

(PREVIOUS) **Tony Stewart helped define NASCAR in the 2000s with a couple of championships and some classic at-track dust-ups with rivals. It was not to be missed.**

BRIAN FRANCE

IF YOU WANT a vivid example of maverick behavior in the world of NASCAR, research the 2004 season. Brian France, having replaced his father, Bill France Jr., as chairman and CEO in October 2003, was altering the sport like few could've imagined.

Of course, he had already done that as a vice president, leading negotiations on the landmark television deal that began in 2001, placing every NASCAR Cup Series race on network TV for the first time. Drivers and teams had more money coming their way than ever before, thanks to that contract.

Just a warmup.

Ramsey Poston was NASCAR's managing director of communications from 2004 to 2011. He calls France "totally underrated as a sports commissioner." Something to that.

In 2004, change was everywhere. Nextel Communications replaced Winston cigarettes as title sponsor for NASCAR's top series, ending a thirty-three-year relationship. Sunoco replaced UNOCAL as the official fuel supplier of NASCAR; UNOCAL or its predecessor brand, Pure, had been the supplier for fifty-three years. The longstanding point system to determine the series champion? Gone, too.

Playoffs had come to NASCAR, with the new Chase for the NASCAR Nextel Cup, which took the top ten drivers after twenty-six races and created a separate point competition for them over the season's last ten events. NASCAR has modified the Chase a couple of times and, now, the last ten races are literally called the NASCAR Playoffs with sixteen drivers in an elimination format.

It was a lot to handle, especially for old-guard fans who longed for the good old days of "smoke 'em if you got 'em," when the series championship was often sewn up at midseason due to a point system that hindered playing catch-up.

"I think Brian was overcriticized because he did things differently from his father," said NASCAR Vice Chairman Mike Helton. "He'll always be underestimated and overcriticized.

"He had a good grasp of the environment it took for NASCAR to be recognized as a major sport and entity. Watching him come up through the ranks, his ingenuity, how he would put the puzzle together and then advance it . . . it was pretty remarkable watching him grow the sport and grow the business of the sport. He didn't mind doing things at the extreme if he thought it made sense. And the playoffs are an example of that."

As a NASCAR vice president, Brian France led negotiations for NASCAR's landmark television rights deal that began in 2001. In 2003, he became the third-generation leader of NASCAR, replacing his father, Bill France Jr., as chairman and CEO.

France worked closely with then-NASCAR Vice President of Licensing Mark Dyer on the Chase concept. Dyer is given considerable credit for the idea. France gets credit for making it happen.

"Brian pushed to get it done," Helton said.

France is glad he did. Across the board, beyond contracts and the frenzy of 2004. Safety initiatives came steadily under his leadership. Key departments had resources to go above and beyond. Diversity finally got a foothold.

"We did the largest deal in the history of sports, in terms of one sponsorship, with the original Nextel deal," France said in 2024, talking about the ten-year, $700,000,000 contract announced in June 2003. "The consolidated TV rights was the key to it all. Those things were all designed to grow the sport.

"With all the things that we set out to do, we didn't move some of them as far as I would have liked but we moved everything, and we were unabashed full-on as a group [about that], led by me. When you think about all we did, it takes your breath away because it wasn't [all] popular, and anytime you change, it's hard."

This was hard: France left NASCAR in 2019 after a 2018 DUI arrest and subsequent leave of absence. He now heads Silver Falcon Capital, a private investment company with headquarters in Charlotte, North Carolina.

"I made a mistake," France told Dale Earnhardt Jr. on his radio show. "It can't happen, a mistake like that. It's on me."

But so are a lot of other things that were not mistakes. Brian France, it seems, will have a complicated legacy.

(continues on page 154)

Brian France weathered plenty of controversy during his 2003 through 2018 time as NASCAR chairman and CEO in the wake of a series of bold moves aimed at growing the sport with the future in mind.

EDDIE GOSSAGE

EDDIE GOSSAGE HAD NO CHOICE but to operate in maverick mode. When he became president of Texas Motor Speedway in 1997, he had a degree from Bruton Smith University in racetrack operation, having studied under the professor of promotion, Humpy Wheeler.

If that didn't prepare him for going over the top, nothing would.

But before Gossage hit his freewheeling, everything's-big-in-Texas stride, he occasionally showed some out-of-the-box PR moxie as an industry public relations type. True story: 1985 Rolex 24 at Daytona. Gossage was handling communications for Miller Brewing Company. He and an associate decided to visit the working press late on the race's Saturday night. Nothing like delivering some cold Millers right after deadline to make some friends. It was working.

That was until Daytona International Speedway representative Larry Balewski noticed some beer drinking going on, over in a corner. Balewski didn't like what he saw: the wrong kind of beverages.

"Guys, this is a Budweiser press box," Balewski informed the group, as he approached with a scowl. Gossage and friends, and their beer, had to leave, booted from the box.

"Larry was right, he was doing the right thing, doing his job," Gossage said. "I went too far."

Said the future master of stretching boundaries, whose role models for his career were Muhammad Ali and Evel Knievel.

In 1989, after leaving Miller—where he led NASCAR Cup Series champion Bobby Allison's PR in 1983—Gossage became a longtime player in Smith's Speedway Motorsports Incorporated empire. Class was in session at Charlotte Motor Speedway, the track Smith opened in 1960. Gossage was the new vice president for communications under Wheeler, the flamboyant—and demanding—track president.

It's safe to say that Gossage absorbed some body blows from Wheeler, a former boxer, as part of his learning process.

"The Charlotte Motor Speedway years were probably the toughest years of my career," Gossage said. "Learned a lot. I learned a lot about what to do. I learned a lot of what not to do. But I learned a lot that helped me.

"I remember an industry association called me one day and congratulated me, saying I had the new record for the longest time working with Humpy."

Wheeler was known for outlandish promotions that involved fake military operations in the infield, pyrotechnics, animals—anything was game. Gossage took it all in and then took it to heart. "Me and Humpy both realized that we thought alike," Gossage said.

Which led to an infamous Gossage gaffe in 1992. To promote the installation of lights at Charlotte Motor Speedway, Gossage had a mock switch installed for the photo opp. Smith hit a lever and sparks flew. Bruton's hair got singed more than a little. Smith, rather than firing Gossage, further embraced him.

Eddie had his template, and what better state to "go big" in than Texas?

"That was the first time I got to spread my wings," Gossage said.

Which translated to ideas like this: cowboy hats, six-shooters, and, for race winners in Victory Lane, monkeys handing out programs to incoming spectators, gifting ponies to Jeff Gordon for his two daughters, a race sponsored by the NRA, and then, there was "Big Hoss."

Big Hoss—a 21,000-square-foot (1,951 sq m) 1080p display—debuted in 2014, looming over the speedway backstretch. Eddie made sure his communications team pointed out that it was bigger than the Lincoln Memorial and weighed more than seven elephants. Humpy used elephants at Charlotte, remember. Of course, he did.

Back in the late 2000s, Gossage was diagnosed with cancer. He beat it, and kept promoting until his 2021 resignation from the speedway. In 2023 he had started treatment for a recurrence. Gossage died in May 2024, only two months after being interviewed for this story. The rambling interview, emotional at times, ended with Gossage offering an invitation to call back if needed.

Damn. Gossage is gone but the beat goes on. His Wikipedia entry is 21 pages long. Eddie Gossage, promoter extraordinaire. Believe it.

Longtime Texas Motor Speedway President Eddie Gossage, a disciple of the great promoter Humpy Wheeler, came up with a good one in 2013: the biggest video screen in the world, "Big Hoss."

Texas-sized confetti was a staple of Texas Motor Speedway President Eddie Gossage's Victory Lane celebrations. Appropriately that Gossage himself was showered at the 2021 NASCAR All-Star Race at TMS, his last race as president.

THE BUSCH BROTHERS

WITH THREE CHAMPIONSHIPS between them in NASCAR's Cup Series and more than three hundred NASCAR national series race wins, brothers Kurt and Kyle Busch have been, unquestionably, the kind of high-speed showmen to make their Las Vegas hometown proud.

In a sport filled with familial legacy—from NASCAR Hall of Fame brothers Bobby and Donnie Allison to Hall of Fame father and son stars Dale Earnhardt and Dale Earnhardt Jr.—the Busch brothers have also turned in championship careers worthy of future enshrinement. The Busches were a new generation of brash and bold talent; outsiders from a relatively new NASCAR market ready to go door to door with the sport's establishment.

The aggressive style both crafted to perfection made these Vegas brothers certain future Hall of Famers, but it also created a unique relationship with their competitors and their fans. Their approach, especially early in their careers, was a blinders-on brazen path—but the results justified their work. And its enduring legacy is something admired by those they battled on track and those in the grandstands who allowed themselves to appreciate the feats.

The support may have been reluctant applause when these brassy twenty-somethings were giving it to the established legends early in their careers, but there's no doubt that as Kurt and Kyle began winning races, and then championships, the admiration grew resoundingly both inside and outside the NASCAR garage.

The talent was unmistakable and their willingness to go door to door with anyone paid off.

Older brother Kurt once famously and figuratively butted heads with one of NASCAR's most established intimidators, Jimmy Spencer—whose nickname was "Mr. Excitement." He rubbed fenders when he needed to and kept track of transgressions on and off track. Similarly, Kurt's younger brother, Kyle, had no problem giving as well as he took, his brash style earning boos at driver introductions—the loudest, most fervent reaction each week, but something all the sport's top drivers experience.

"When you're young and you start beating up on the guys that have been here for a while, people don't really take well to that so you're not really well liked, and especially doing it the brash way that I did early on," the two-time champion Kyle Busch recalled with a grin. "It certainly got some more eyeballs on my name. But as I've gotten a little bit older and matured and not won as often, people are like, 'That guy used to win all the time, so I'm going to pull for him, I want him to win. Let's see him win some more.' It turns the tables for sure.

"I remember how many times Jeff Gordon got booed after a win in the late nineties and then his last win he had at Martinsville, the crowd went nuts. Times change and the tables turn."

The most important element to all this, however, was that the Busch brothers have won, and won often.

WHILE DRIVING FOR legendary racing team owner Jack Roush early in his career, Kurt Busch earned fourteen of his thirty-four career victories and the 2004 NASCAR Cup Series championship. He claimed the sport's most acclaimed trophy in the 2017 Daytona 500 in his first race driving for NASCAR Hall of Famer Tony Stewart's team. And he closed out his career in 2022 having won a race in nine previous consecutive seasons for three different teams.

"I'm very happy, complacent," Kurt Busch said when announcing his retirement in 2023. "There's nothing I look back on and regret about having this opportunity at the top level of NASCAR."

Kyle Busch, seven years younger than Kurt, has two NASCAR Cup Series championships, one representing one of the most incredible comebacks in series history and further proof of the gumption he boasted. After severely breaking his leg competing in a NASCAR Xfinity Series race the day before the 2015 Daytona 500, Busch missed eleven NASCAR Cup Series races. Yet, he still was able to return to competition, win five races—including one only five weeks after his medical clearance—en route to his first series championship.

As impressively, Busch has earned an unprecedented 280 victories in a combination of NASCAR's three premier series: NASCAR Cup Series (63), Xfinity Series (102), and Craftsman Truck Series (115). His totals in Xfinity and the trucks are records, and the only other driver with more two hundred wins in all NASCAR national series is the legend Richard Petty, who won two hundred times in his NASCAR Cup career.

A combination of awesome natural talent and the exceptional nerve to excel against the odds—flourishing with that fine line combination of aggression and finesse—have made Kurt and Kyle Busch among the sport's all-time best.

"It certainly has been [amazing] and grateful to Mom and Dad for getting us to this point and pressing us as hard as they did growing up, and getting us to learn everything they did about the cars and having a good car sense," Kyle Busch said. "I think that's kinda what brought us on as well and successful as we've been, just that dedication to what we love and the passion for our sport. It has been great."

Kurt Busch won the 2004 NASCAR Cup Series championship and the 2017 Daytona 500. He retired in 2024. The Hall of Fame beckons.

Kyle Busch, younger brother of Kurt Busch, won NASCAR Cup Series championships in 2015 and '19. He wasn't exactly the most popular driver, to say the least—except with kids; his cars were sponsored by M&Ms for years. He has acquired a fine nickname: "Rowdy." He prefers the one he dreamed up: "KFB."

Long before there was a Jim Hunter bobblehead, Hunter was already involved in motorsports, as an auto racing journalist and racetrack public relations representative.

JIM HUNTER

JIM HUNTER was an original and one of the most visible, long-time lieutenants in the NASCAR army, working for the sanctioning body and its sister company, the International Speedway Corporation (ISC), from 1983 through 2010.

For most of his career that spanned six decades, he went back and forth between the two organizations, which was easy to do if you had the chops. Prior to a 2019 merger, which was actually a NASCAR purchase of ISC, NASCAR was a private business owned and operated by the France family, whereas ISC was publicly traded and owned thirteen racetracks—and controlled by the France family.

Hunter was ready to serve when and where needed. And boy did he serve, after a stint working public relations for Dodge that was key in prepping for the big time.

- Early 1980s: Public relations director at Darlington Raceway and Talladega Superspeedway
- 1983: NASCAR vice president of administration
- 1993: Darlington Raceway president and ISC vice president
- 2001: NASCAR vice president of communications

He returned for the final NASCAR stint in '01 because Bill France Jr. asked him to. Besides, he had grown bored as Darlington's president. "You can only play so much golf."

There was no boredom in Daytona Beach and not nearly as much time for a quick nine. At least not for a while; 2001 was going to be a landmark year for NASCAR, in so many ways. It started with the Daytona 500.

NASCAR was holding its first Winston Cup Series race under a new television contract that paid gazillions and consolidated coverage of Cup Series races onto *real* networks. FOX (sixteen) and NBC (fifteen) covered most of the races, followed by TBS (seven), and ABC (one).

Whereupon, with that stage as the backdrop, Dale Earnhardt, arguably NASCAR's greatest driver, died in a last-lap crash. Just like that, NASCAR's safety record was under scrutiny. The fans—hell, the world—wanted to know what happened.

A six-month investigation ensued alongside record TV ratings. Hunter ran point on PR for that deal. Findings were announced in August and safety improvements started coming.

This shot is from the Sonny Bono years, also known as the years in the early eighties when Jim Hunter served as NASCAR Vice President of Administration.

So did the media, like never before. Hunter was there and that was a good thing.

He became NASCAR's main at-track spokesman during the 2000s, especially when the subject was serious. Known for his downhome style of spin that sometimes danced on the edge of credibility, Hunter also was the media's go-to guy when there was no room for spin. In those settings, Hunter gave it to you straight. Somewhat.

He had so many stories of his years in the industry. Some are printable. Yarns about his pre-NASCAR colorful past as an editor at the *Columbia* (South Carolina) *Record* and a sportswriter at the *Atlanta Journal-Constitution* were the best, stories involving a lot of whiskey and a bit of the "wacky tobacky" as he loved to say just to see people react.

How about the time he and some fellow journalists were in full-toke mode, talking about outer space he said, and Hunter took a break to get a soda? The hotel's machine didn't work—the soda can jammed and Hunter decided to hit the cement and stretch his arm up into the machine. About that time, a well-known team owner walked down the hallway.

"Evening, Jim."

"Hey, pal."

Without doubt, Hunter's most memorable tale happened in 1983 when he was the public relations director at Talladega and he decided to drive the pace car to Atlanta, to meet friends at a honky-tonk. At least that's one story. His widow, Ann Hunter, swears he was coming home since it was already getting late.

Whatever the planned destination, Hunter hauled ass out of the racetrack, hammered. Made it to the edge of the property, where the quick left/right led you toward I-10, toward Atlanta and all the honky-tonks you could handle. No interstate—or home—for our boy Jimbo that night. He flipped the car and was taken to the hospital to recuperate from multiple injuries.

The car was totaled. "Big Bill" France, still on the scene but not the front lines, fired Hunter. Bill France Jr. told Hunter, "Fuck it. He'll forget about it in a few days." Bill told Jim to stay away from the office for a few days. He did, Senior forgot, and Hunter kept working.

He didn't keep drinking.

That was it, and if he needed a reminder of why he shouldn't drink, he would reach into his top right desk drawer, and pull out an old Polaroid of him in a hospital bed, looking like he had, well, been in a car wreck.

"That was a wake-up call—a huge wake-up call," said Jim's son, Scott Hunter. "It really was cold turkey for him. He quit drinking and got everything together."

Hunter, who died in October 2010 after a brief battle against lung cancer, became a NASCAR celebrity in the last decade of his life. Oh, he had been *the man* before, as president of Darlington, or in his previous NASCAR executive stints. This was different. On top of sellout crowds, millions of people now watched *every* NASCAR Cup Series race on television, which meant millions of people got to know the old guy with the downhome drawl named Jim Hunter.

He even developed a look. The ever-present mustard yellow "NASCAR 48" ball cap became known as the "Hunter hat." Brown-and-white Oxford-style golf shoes completed things. He had his own bobblehead, with the trademark cigarette in his right fist.

"When he spoke, and the way he looked someone in the eye and delivered the message, you knew that this was coming from the highest [NASCAR] authority," said Ramsey Poston, NASCAR's managing director of communications under Hunter from 2004 to 2011.

"You knew that Jim Hunter was on your side, giving you information that was important and accurate. And he had a way with his unpolished delivery, kind of casual. He knew how to put color into any issue or situation."

Regarding spin, Hunter mastered the art but often would just avoid it, offering a limited response that made it clear: end of discussion. But when questions allowed him to elaborate . . . he was golden.

"It was like he was a conductor and it was a perfect symphony, eloquence, man," said Russell Branham, Darlington's PR director when Hunter was president.

Hunter had a special kinship with Kerry Tharp, who rose to senior communications director before leaving to become Darlington's president, Hunter's old job. Before NASCAR, Tharp led sports communications at the University of South Carolina, Hunter's alma mater, where he played football as a 130-pound (59 kg) wide receiver.

"Jim was one of the smartest, craftiest people I ever worked with," Tharp said. "A real spin doctor."

George Pyne was NASCAR's chief operating officer, overseeing PR, when Hunter arrived from Darlington.

"Jim was one hundred percent a maverick," Pyne said. "At NASCAR, so much changed during my time there and one of the great things about Jim, and Bill France Jr. too, is that they embraced change, brought in a lot of young people, were respectful of tradition but were really open to new ideas. That's what made Jim special to me. He kind of bridged the old and the new."

No doubt. Hunter loved working with young people, saying it kept him young. As far as openness, Tracey Judd can vouch for that in a most personal fashion. Hunter hired Judd for his PR team in 2002. She rose to a director position before retiring in 2015. Judd is a gay woman. Hunter could not have cared less.

Some people in NASCAR did care. When Hunter got wind of that, he said this, "So let me get this straight . . . She likes women. Well, so do I! Who gives a fuck?"

Said Judd, "He put you at ease. I cherish every moment I had with him, all the highs and all the lows. He's on my personal Mount Rushmore of mentors."

Pyne spent most of his NASCAR years immersed, side by side, with Hunter, in serious developments within the sport: Earnhardt's death, controversy about the new point system, a new title sponsor to replace entrenched Winston, a new Cup Series car. But when asked about those days and Jimbo, Pyne emphasized this.

"I just liked Jim as a person."

(continues on page 162)

Jim Hunter left his position as Darlington Raceway president in 2001 to head NASCAR's ramped-up public relations efforts.

CLAIRE B. LANG

CLAIRE B. LANG is the daughter of an Olympic long jumper so let's assume her 2001 career leap came naturally.

And she did stick the landing.

Lang has been the most popular radio voice for NASCAR fans this century, except for the late Motor Racing Network legend Barney Hall. Between 2001 and 2023, she became the voice of new-fangled satellite radio coverage of NASCAR, first for XM, then for post-merger SiriusXM, putting in hour after hour at race after race for year after year. On a race weekend, she was everywhere, interviewing thousands of drivers, owners, and fans over the course of each season to deliver the consummate coverage.

In 2001, satellite radio was just starting to get hot, soon to get hotter. NASCAR's listening audience was committed to traditional "terrestrial" radio. This satellite deal was weird, especially since you had to pay for it. Things changed quickly for the industry, and for Lang. XM, then SiriusXM, became a destination for NASCAR fans. Lang, with a solid radio background, became one of the first female sports radio *hosts*. People must know: Lang cares more about being noticed for her work than her gender. Such is the burden of a pioneer.

Lang and SiriusXM parted ways before the 2024 season—bad deal for NASCAR fans—which only reinforced her rep. People missed her show; it was called *Dialed In*, and that she was, mercurial with the microphone, a 5 foot 1 inch, one-hundred-pound (1 m 53 cm) force of nature doing laps around the garage. If broadcasting was a sport, she would've been drug tested. Results would've shown high levels of dedication.

A NASCAR Cup Series race or event meant Claire B. had to be in the vicinity. The infield media center, pit road, Victory Lane, in the garage, in the grandstands, at every preseason media op and postseason awards show. Claire was there, from Watkins Glen to the Waldorf Astoria.

Back in 2001, Lang came into a sport experiencing unprecedented visibility. A new landmark TV rights deal debuted with Dale Earnhardt's death in the Daytona 500. The sport spiked in popularity. Make what you will of that.

But the spike was real and so was Claire B. Lang. The garage was a madhouse on race weekends in the 2000s. In the middle of the madness, Lang became a star.

"I was so excited about the canvas that I had, to tell the story of NASCAR," Lang said. "It was a canvas to paint on. But I had to do it all on my own. It was hard. Long hours. First one to arrive in the media center and the last to leave, a lot of times."

Her father, 1956 Olympic silver medalist John Bennett, was especially proud when she received the 2021 CYNOPSIS Top Women in Media Award for Game Changing On-Air Talent.

"The Olympic motto is 'Faster, Higher, Stronger' and Claire certainly exemplifies that in all she has achieved in her life and career," Bennett said. "She is a gold medal daughter!"

Medal winner, game changer, maverick. All the same thing when you come right down to it, in this case.

Said Lang, "I always just wanted to do the best job possible."

From 2001 to 2023, reporter Claire B. Lang became a fixture on XM and SIRIUS XM satellite radio channels. Which meant she was a fixture in the NASCAR garages and media centers.

TONY STEWART

IT MAY SURPRISE MANY in his massive fandom—or maybe not—to know that NASCAR Hall of Famer Tony Stewart's amazing ability to win at every professional level of racing may have actually been rooted in something far more elementary than a race car.

Playing the game Monopoly as a kid.

"I grew up in a very competitive family," Stewart explained. "One of the things we did was, every Friday night, we played board games. My sister and I played with our parents and our parents never let us win. There was none of this 'BS' participation ribbons and all that stuff.

"Played Monopoly, all the classic board games of the seventies but the important part was that our parents never let us win. If we won, we had to earn it. And they didn't give us a break. We all were cutthroat and I think that just kind of builds your character."

Of course, there was a whole lot of natural talent and uncommon motivation behind his racing legend too, but the USAC, IndyCar, and NASCAR champion absolutely believes the mindset established early in his life at least contributed to the competitive difference. Character was something Stewart established his illustrious career upon.

Informed opinion was never a problem for Stewart and he was never one to hold back—from challenging a race series or a fellow driver. Certainly, the racing media.

A hugely popular driver, both in the grandstands and even in the paddock among his competitors, Stewart quickly established himself as a leader. He developed great rapport not only with those he competed against but also with series executives. Stewart instinctively understood that making the sport viable and popular depended on a good relationship among the garage, front offices, and drivers.

And he never held back.

Now a track and race series owner—as well as a team owner in many disciplines and races—Stewart says he has developed a unique and comprehensive understanding of the sport, beyond his days when his greatest responsibility was wheeling a car to victory.

"I wouldn't make a very good politician, and I never have," Stewart said with a smile. "I think one of the best things I did was owning a racetrack and owning a race series. It helped me understand the challenges NASCAR and IndyCar and the NHRA go through, so it's given me a different perspective where I appreciate what they have to go through. But, there's still ways a lot of these sanctioning bodies do things I don't necessarily always agree with. I think that's human nature too."

Part of what made Stewart such a hugely popular competitor was his knack for playing it straight. There has never been any question as to where he stands when it comes to doing right by racer or by fan.

Sure, there were those moments on track when a helmet throw or physical confrontation got the attention of a competitor. A microphone in Stewart's face immediately after a dustup or incident on track was bound to give a sound bite for the ages. It was all part of what endeared Stewart to the fans and gave him a sort of "man of the people" vibe.

After being eliminated from a victory in one of Talladega (Alabama) Superspeedway's famous "big ones," the sidelined Stewart famously suggested—with a straight face—to the national television audience that maybe the most compelling way to run a race on those high banks would be using a figure-8 design and, beyond that, running half the laps backwards. He "apologized" for the field not crashing more cars and said perhaps they should extend the race so at least 50 percent of the cars were out.

Only Stewart could get away with that kind of post-race reaction. That's because he carried the respect of the officials and his fellow competitors. And the fans loved their modern-day maverick.

The racing media was a particular source of give-and-take for Stewart, more so than most any other driver during this time. What was perceived as a "dumb" or unnecessary question from a reporter was immediately seized upon by Stewart, whether in a private group setting or a more formal press conference. Using sarcasm like a lost art, Stewart would gladly settle in for whatever query came his way. Fellow drivers sitting alongside Stewart would put their hands over their smiles, eager to hear how he would dress down the inquiring reporter.

And although he would shake his head and toss out some zingers, Stewart seemed to enjoy the debate. It was passion. The same kind that distinguished him both in a car and in any review of his great work.

Stewart earned sixty-two wins in NASCAR's three national series including forty-nine in the Cup Series—sixteenth best all-time. A three-time NASCAR Cup Series champion (2002,

Tony Stewart brought a racer's mentality, and the requisite fiery personality, to NASCAR, winning three NASCAR Cup Series championships.

Tony Stewart, in the style of IndyCar star Hélio Castroneves, became a NASCAR "Spider-Man" with his own celebratory, front-straight fence-climbing.

Tony Stewart seemed especially at home rubbing fenders at short tracks like Bristol Motor Speedway during his NASCAR career. Sometimes, a scuffle ensued. Ask Matt Kenseth or Jeff Gordon about this.

'05, '11), his final title run was one of the most inspired, most entertaining in history. Winless during the 2011 regular season, the owner-driver claimed five of the ten playoff race trophies en route to championship, calling his shot in the championship finale race.

Before his NASCAR career, he earned three IndyCar series victories and the 1997 title. And he was famously the first driver in history to win the United States Auto Club (USAC) Triple Crown, claiming the national Midget, Sprint, and Silver Crown divisions all in the same season (1995).

The wins and the championships are what may put Stewart in the halls of fame and record books. But it's absolutely his maverick style and spirit that won over competitors and fans and make Stewart that one-of-a-kind champion. It wasn't just that Stewart won a lot, but it was the way he won, the way he raced. And that kind of unfettered, heartfelt passion may never be seen again in racing's rank and file.

"We definitely went against the grain on a lot of things in this sport," Stewart acknowledged. "And still, to this day, we still push against the grain with a lot of these guys. My time in the sport as a driver, we got to see a lot of changes in the time I drove . . . just a lot of things that happened and changed in the sport.

"I jokingly tell people, don't confuse bravery with stupidity. I was always raised to speak my mind and stand up for what I believed in. So, yes, if I thought something wasn't being done right, I would say something. And if I was wrong on it and they explained it to me and I was wrong, then I owned up to it.

"There were a lot of times I was right but, because of other variables, they had to do it a different way still. But I learned a lot and that's made me better.

"I don't know if I would classify myself that way [as a maverick], but I definitely understand why others might. I definitely think it's fair."

(LEFT) **Tony Stewart won the first of his three NASCAR Cup Series championships in 2002, clinching with a twentieth-place finish at the Homestead-Miami Speedway finale.**

(BELOW) **Indiana native Tony Stewart realized a childhood dream in 2005—a victory at Indianapolis Motor Speedway, in the Brickyard 400. So, of course, he kissed the yard of bricks at the start-finish line, to celebrate.**

CHAD KNAUS

CHAD KNAUS IS COMFORTABLE with his status as one of the most inventive rule benders—and rule breakers—in NASCAR history. And why not? Hasn't hurt his career.

Knaus was inducted into the NASCAR Hall of Fame in January 2024. A month later, he was asked how it felt to be in the same conversation as other legendary maverick crew chiefs who caught NASCAR's ire on multiple occasions. Knaus has become a modern-day outlaw and has decided he likes it.

"Ohhh, you're damn right," Knaus said.

Here's what distinguishes Knaus, and the main reason he has made it to the Hall of Fame: He won seven NASCAR Cup Series championships as crew chief for driver Jimmie Johnson.

Knaus won eighty-two races as a crew chief, all with Hendrick Motorsports and eighty-one were with Johnson. The last win came with young star William Byron in 2020. Knaus is third all-time in crew chief victories, behind Dale Inman and Leonard Wood. Byron won the 2024 Daytona 500. Knaus was watching. He's now Hendrick's vice president of competition.

Back to the rep that Knaus came by honestly in NASCAR. He was suspended four times, in 2001, '06, '07, and '12 and twice paid $100,000 fines. The fourth suspension was rescinded. The violation most fans recall was at the 2006 Daytona 500. An illegal rear-window adjustment found after qualifying got Knaus tossed for three races.

Knaus, from Rockford, Illinois, honed his cheatin' skills on Midwest short tracks in the 1970s and '80s.

"I love [the image]," he said. "It's where I came from, that's what you did, in motorsports in the Midwest in the seventies and eighties. Everybody wanted to have a better car and that's how you got your advantage. If you had a better car, you had a better opportunity to win races.

"My approach was, always, don't do anything that's blatantly illegal, right? We always took the opportunity to—and always still do—try to find an advantage. And when you find that advantage . . . you got to be willing to take a little bit of risk."

Knaus stands as the latest in the lineage of risk takers that is dotted with names like Smokey Yunick and Gary Nelson. Is he the last?

"Boy, there's not as many [left]," Knaus said. "Things are tighter, restrictions on motorsports, in general, are so much tighter. We had a lot more freedoms [in the past] and I think that freedom bred that type of mentality, which was just fantastic."

Wily Chad Knaus was crew chief for all of Jimmie Johnson's seven NASCAR Cup Series championship seasons. Good chance a few rules were bent and/or broken during that time. Just a hunch.

Jimmie Johnson and Chad Knaus teamed up to win seven NASCAR Cup Series championships. Here they celebrate the last one in 2016, at Homestead-Miami Speedway.

CLASH
Coca-Cola
TOYOTA
REDDICK
KYLE BUSCH
18
CAMRY

CHAPTER 8

THE 2010s TO 2020s

NEW RACES AND NEW FACES

This book's last chapter covers NASCAR's latest chapter, one rampant with change albeit with a noticeable tweak from the 2000s when outreach to new fans partially backfired.

TWO DECADES BACK, the advent of new races, new rules, new sponsors, new leadership, and a new point system were too much to handle for many who longed for days gone by. Too much change too soon was a familiar refrain. Core fans felt forsaken.

Undaunted, NASCAR has mashed the gas again, only this time making sure traditional fans are top of mind.

You've had new, adventurous races in Chicago and Los Angeles. But the adventure has also come to Bristol Motor Speedway with three years of dirt shows and to long-shuttered short track North Wilkesboro, reopened, refurbished, and home to the NASCAR All-Star Race in 2023–'24.

NASCAR touts this duality, as well it should. Looking ahead and looking back simultaneously isn't easy. But it's admirable. No one can say the sanctioning body isn't trying.

Diversity is helping, not only via owner Michael Jordan and driver Bubba Wallace being on the scene but also with initiatives throughout the industry. NASCAR is, indeed, starting to reflect the multicultured face of America. If you don't like that, well, let's just say you better get used to it.

Competition is helping, but that remains—and always will be—a work in progress. The evolution of the NASCAR Cup Series car continues, albeit overshadowed in the public eye by things like rubbin' fenders on downtown Chicago streets.

Yes, this isn't your grandfather's NASCAR, and there's not a damn thing wrong with that.

The Los Angeles Coliseum, all dressed up and ready to race.

NASCAR'S BOLD INITIATIVES

NASCAR'S RAPID-FIRE DELIVERY of new races in recent years for the NASCAR Cup Series has been bold. And it's been a break from the past, but only the recent past. NASCAR history is all about taking chances, doing something different.

Like racing in the 1940s on a 4-mile course consisting of 2 miles of hard-packed Atlantic shoreline sand and 2 miles of half-ass asphalt, also known as State Road A1A.

Like building a 2.5-mile track out of North Florida nothingness in Daytona Beach, Florida, in 1957 to '59, with banking sure to make drivers pee their coveralls, then go out to a beachside watering hole to bitch about the place and NASCAR President Bill France Sr.

So maybe a few new races aren't exactly revolutionary.

Still, it sure has seemed that way.

Simply put, NASCAR hasn't messed around here, with a two-pronged reach out to new fans and core fans. Translation: young and old.

With a Chi-Town skyline as the backdrop, Kyle Larson, in the number five Hendrick Motorsports Chevy, leads the pack through a tight turn during the 2023 Chicago Street Course race.

- From 2021 to '23, red clay was dumped on top of the 5.33-mile Bristol Motor Speedway oval for the spring NASCAR Cup Series race, the first Cup race on dirt since the sixties. It was okay, but the race is back to concrete.

"Was the Bristol dirt a success? I guess that depends on how you view a success," said journalist Jordan Bianchi of *The Athletic*. "For three years it gave new life and energy to the Bristol spring race, which was certainly lagging a little bit."

- From 2022 to '24, the Busch Light Clash at the Coliseum was held at, well, the Los Angeles Coliseum, site of the first Super Bowl, some of O. J. Simpson's greatest afternoons, some really bad Los Angeles Rams seasons—and the Olympics. This race started as the Busch Clash in 1979 and for years was known as the Bud Shootout, always held at Daytona International Speedway. Might not return, but that's cool.

BEN KENNEDY, NASCAR's bright, young senior vice president of racing development, is at the forefront of these changes. He was a racer first, competing in the NASCAR Camping World Truck Series and Xfinity Series, winning a race in the latter.

Correction: First, Ben Kennedy was NASCAR Executive Vice Chair Lesa France Kennedy's son, Bill France Jr.'s grandson, Bill Sr.'s great-grandson. Of course, he looks—and sounds—like the future boss, at the age of thirty-two starting the 2024 season.

Regarding the Clash moving, Kennedy preaches the big-picture approach. NASCAR has been chasing LA fans for years. The Coliseum is big picture—and wide net.

"We felt like it's an opportunity for us to try something different, to try something new, and go to a major market like Los Angeles," Kennedy said. "We put our heads together on a number of different options and LA came to the forefront. It's a massive market for us from a fan perspective; there are more NASCAR fans in the LA DMA [designated market area] than anywhere else in the world, which surprises a lot of people.

"The Clash races have been opportunities to bring new fans out to what is a temporary track in downtown Los Angeles and give them the opportunity to sample a version of what NASCAR could be like. This has also been an opportunity to test some new things that are novel for us, like a pre-race concert and a halftime show."

Reviews have been mixed about the quality of the competition on the ¼-mile oval. Those reviews may be missing the point.

Kelly Crandall, co-author of the 2023 book *NASCAR 75 Years*, one of the newer, younger journalists now covering NASCAR, said, "To me, the racing hasn't been that good, I think, but LA is more like a pep rally to hype the season. It's a party where a race breaks out."

Added Bianchi, "NASCAR brought the race to the people of Los Angeles, with a purpose-built track inside a football stadium. Before, you would never even think that could be done, but they did it."

- In 2023–'24, the NASCAR Chicago Street Race brought the Cup Series into the Windy City's downtown and, despite terrible weather, it was a hit. NASCAR's contract with the city runs through '25. Going into the '24 race, NASCAR was counting on good weather the second time around—and an even bigger hit.

"With Chicago, I'd say we took a very similar tack to Los Angles," Kennedy said. "Another big opportunity. Literally, bringing our product to the people. We had never had a street race in the Cup Series, for seventy-five years. Now, we're not going to have fifteen street courses on the Cup Series schedule in the future, but we could have two or three."

- Also in 2023–'24, the NASCAR All-Star race was held at storied North Wilkesboro Speedway, which closed in 1996 when it was dropped from the Cup Series schedule. The track reopened in 2010–'11 for a few lower-level events, but then closed for good—or so it looked. Speedway Motorsports Incorporated, which owns the short track, resurrected, and then refurbished, the place. It's a back-to-the-roots race. Some old red-and-white Winston cigarette sponsor signage remains, a nod to history. The All-Star race used to be called "The Winston." The trophy is a still. A nod-off to history.

Kyle Larson celebrates after winning the NASCAR Cup Series All-Star Race at reopened North Wilkesboro Speedway in 2023—a time-travel experience for competitors and fans alike.

"Conversely to LA and Chicago, North Wilkesboro is tailored for the avid fans," Kennedy added.

North Wilkesboro has somewhat usurped the higher-profile new venues—for now.

Covering the 2023 all-star event was "like going in a time machine to a bygone era," Bianchi said. "Nobody thought the track would actually come back from the dead. And then it actually came back. There was this incredible feeling [at the 2023 race] of 'this is what it should be.' It was just remarkable."

Collectively, including the Bristol dirt, the new races represent a new reality, in contrast to the sport's traditional approach.

"NASCAR has embraced the idea that the schedule doesn't have to be written in concrete," said journalist and author Greg Engle.

Long overdue, you gotta think.

Leave it to NASCAR President Steve Phelps to knot the bowtie here.

"We are not changing just for the sake of change," Phelps said. "We want to nurture existing fans and bring new fans into the fold. And the key piece to all this is the fans.

"Bold and innovative thinking—that's what this sport needs."

(continues on page 176)

KERRY THARP

Kerry Tharp settled into his role as "The Commander" most visibly when moderating NASCAR press conferences.

KERRY THARP CAME TO NASCAR already accomplished in the world of sports. Twenty-six years in intercollegiate athletics public relations—he rose to the position of associate athletics director for media relations at the University of South Carolina—will do that for you.

Those accomplishments notwithstanding, Tharp arrived at NASCAR as a novice. He retired in 2023 as one of the sport's most beloved people within the industry, first in NASCAR communications and then, starting in 2016, as president of Darlington Raceway.

He even acquired his own nickname: "The Commander."

"I remember when a bunch of our NASCAR PR folks were leaving the famous 21 Club in New York one year after a champion's week event and another PR guy yelled out that I should be called 'Commander Competition' since I worked on the competition side," Tharp said.

"It stuck."

Soon it was simply "Commander" and that was that. Commander it would be for Tharp as he, again, climbed a ladder to senior director of PR at NASCAR before moving over to the racetrack side of the business.

And throughout, he commanded his own way, weaving a pragmatic, corporate sensibility with a good ol' boy approach.

It worked. Just like former NASCAR Vice President Mark Dyer, who initially hired Tharp for a licensing PR job in the spring of 2005, said it would. That job only lasted a few months before the main PR department snagged him.

"I brought kind of a fresh perspective," Tharp said. "I'd been around really big events and had also been around the media for years. College sports was a great training ground for NASCAR."

The Commander leaves a legacy of professionalism—and memories of two classic press conference introductions.

Not long after joining the PR department, Tharp was assigned to moderate a "presser" with three major players—former Daytona 500 champion Ward Burton, his crew chief, Chris Carrier, and car owner, Larry McClure. Tharp, learning quickly but learning still, knew Ward Burton . . . and *only* Ward Burton.

And so, this intro: "We're joined now by former Daytona 500 champion Ward Burton and . . . a couple other guys."

Classic.

Next season, Mike Wallace raced his way into the Daytona 500, in a car sponsored by the Miccosukee gaming operation. Uh-oh.

Tharp: "We're joined by Mike Wallace, driver of the number O-nine Micca . . . Mika . . . Micco . . . uh, uh."

Wallace jumped in: "Mic-co-su-kee Re-sorts."

Gaffes and a few laughs, but extremely small stuff in the big picture of Kerry Tharp and NASCAR. His second career proceeded swimmingly; his personality played a huge role.

"He charms and disarms," said his former NASCAR PR boss Ramsey Poston. "One of Kerry Tharp's greatest attributes is he's an excellent listener. He listens, understands the assignment, and then knows how to carry it out with aplomb, his touch, his own style."

Tharp was the maestro moderator in media centers for more than fifteen years, always opening with what became his signature: "We're going to roll right into our post-race press conference."

Kerry Tharp, during his days with NASCAR, gives Joey Logano some sage public relations advice. Not sure Logano listened.

Darlington Raceway President Kerry Tharp presents the Johnny Mantz Southern 500 trophy to Erik Jones in 2022.

And on it rolled. Working out of NASCAR's Research and Development Center in Concord, North Carolina, he was the media's daily go-to for news about the "on-track product." And at the races, Tharp was in his glory, particularly when weekend PR staffing included other veterans; he called them "The Varsity."

"All Kerry did was blossom and grow and become kind of the legendary NASCAR guy," Poston said.

Tharp's move to Darlington, back in the state where he had earned his PR chops, came at the perfect time, perfect place.

"I've poured my heart and soul into serving our fans at Darlington, and they've in turn embraced my wife, Debbie, and our family as one of their own," Tharp said when he retired.

"My biggest love affair with NASCAR was always with the people. I loved the people. I enjoyed being at the racetrack, being in the garage, in the media center. I just enjoyed all of it."

Martin Truex Jr. won the 2017 NASCAR Cup Series championship driving for a single-car team, Furniture Row Racing, based not in North Carolina but In Denver, Colorado. Mold-breaking everywhere by that memorable group.

FURNITURE ROW RACING

EVEN YEARS BEYOND that celebratory fall evening at Homestead-Miami Speedway when Martin Truex Jr. triumphantly hoisted the 2017 NASCAR Cup Series championship trophy, the former champ still breaks into a huge grin and proclaims of his title time at Furniture Row Racing, "I think about it every single day."

It is an achievement seldom seen in modern day NASCAR, a single-car team operating thousands of miles from the Charlotte beating heart of the sport—not just claiming the championship, but earning it in a dominant way. That is the legacy of Denver's Furniture Row Racing.

It was NASCAR's modern-day "mic drop."

A mixed group of loyal trophy believers at Furniture Row Racing—several of the sport's longtime stalwarts turning wrenches to a relatively unknown crew chief from Canada to a talented driver looking to capitalize on a second chance—made it happen. Colorado businessman Barney Visser brought together all these highly determined, variably motivated talents and gave them a place to flourish—off the NASCAR grid but decidedly in the NASCAR heart.

Not surprisingly, for a team owner fully committed to operating out of his own state—even if it was a pair of time zones beyond the NASCAR epicenter—Visser was not only open to doing things a little differently, he insisted on such.

And after a dozen years of the team methodically working its way toward full-time competition, Furniture Row answered all those who may have underestimated the drive of this group in pursuit of NASCAR's most valued trophy.

While the sport's other marquee teams had massive technological support systems, scores of pedigreed crew members, and high-profile drivers, Furniture Row exceeded with brains, heart, and gumption. It did more with less, week after week. After week.

(ABOVE LEFT) **Martin Truex Jr. won the 2017 NASCAR Cup Series championship driving for a single-car team, Furniture Row Racing, based not in North Carolina, but In Denver, Colorado. Mold-breaking everywhere by that memorable group.**

(ABOVE RIGHT) **Martin Truex Jr. celebrates in Victory Lane after winning the 2017 Monster Energy NASCAR Cup Series championship.**

Furniture Row's 2017 championship crew chief, Canadian Cole Pearn earned cult-like status in the sport for his unconventional manner and ultracompetitive zeal. Unlike the more formally outfitted crew chiefs, Pearn wore a simple T-shirt emblazoned with nothing but the team logo and outworked, outstrategized, and outran the entire more formal establishment. In his tenure, he oversaw seventeen of the company's eighteen wins and is the first Canadian-born crew chief to earn a NASCAR Cup Series victory, much less a championship.

It was an equally compelling triumph for the talented Truex, a two-time NASCAR Busch Series champion with the Dale Earnhardt Inc. (DEI) organization, who had some early success but truly shined his star in that eight-win trophy-hoisting season, besting the powerhouse teams such as Hendrick Motorsports, Stewart-Haas Racing, and even Furniture Row's technical partner, Joe Gibbs Racing.

It turned out to be an elaborate curtain call for Visser's humble, lower-budget Furniture Row Racing team that closed shop following the next season (2018), thirteen years after its first start in NASCAR's marquee series—a single race at Phoenix Raceway in 2005 with Colorado driver Jerry Robertson, making his series debut at the age of forty-three. He started forty-third of forty-three cars and finished forty-first, the car retiring early with engine problems.

An assortment of more familiar NASCAR names followed Robertson in the team's subsequent partial seasons of competition from 2006 to 2010, from former Busch Grand National champion Joe Nemechek to another multiseries talent, Kenny Wallace.

Another Busch Grand National champion, Regan Smith earned the team's first victory in a fittingly dramatic scenario—an overtime win over perennial race favorite Carl Edwards at NASCAR's historically tough Darlington (South Carolina) Raceway.

Former NASCAR Cup Series champion Kurt Busch drove a partial schedule for the team in 2012–'13 before turning over the wheel to Truex in 2015. The Truex and Pearn combination won seventeen of the team's eighteen races—highlighted by the 2017 championship—and along with Visser and the Furniture Row Racing team, contributed an absolutely amazing and unlikely chapter to the NASCAR lore.

"It was just a different kind of way of doing things," Truex said. "And thinking back on that team and what we were able to accomplish, it's just amazing.

"We had an ace up our sleeve with the collaboration with JGR and Toyota, so we had some more room to be creative and kind of take gambles and risks and still not have the big corporate banner.

"It was definitely interesting to see how it all worked and to think back and just compare it to what we do now.

"It was just a band of outlaws, so to speak. It was definitely fun."

(continues on page 180)

23XI RACING

YOU HAVE TO LIKE THE TEAM NAME, to start. Roman numerals aren't a typical component of a NASCAR brand, especially when they're combined with the jersey number of the greatest basketball player in history who also happens to be the team co-owner. The fact that the Romans represent the No. 11 car of a three-time Daytona 500 champion, the other co-owner . . . even better.

It reads 23XI. It's pronounced "twenty-three-eleven" racing. That was the story on September 21, 2020, when Michael Jordan hand-checked the COVID pandemic, joining Denny Hamlin to announce they were starting a new NASCAR Cup Series team, with 2021 the first season of competition. Michael Jordan became the only current Black team owner in the NASCAR Cup Series, and he immediately hired Bubba Wallace, the only Black driver in the series, as his team's first driver.

This was monumental. And after a closer look, it made total sense. Jordan, after all, is from North Carolina, the heart of NASCAR racing. He also appears to be set financially. At least that's what we've heard.

"Growing up in North Carolina, my parents would take my brothers, sisters, and me to races, and I've been a NASCAR fan my whole life," Jordan said at the announcement. "The opportunity to own my own racing team in partnership with my friend, Denny Hamlin, and to have Bubba Wallace driving for us, is very exciting for me. Historically, NASCAR has struggled with diversity and there have been few Black owners. The timing seemed perfect, as NASCAR is evolving and embracing social change more and more.

"In addition to the recent commitment and donations I have made to combat systemic racism, I see this as a chance to educate a new audience and open more opportunities for Black people in racing."

From the get-go, it was clear that Jordan would not be another rich, absentee sports team owner, and that 23XI was a serious venture by the six-time NBA champion. A foundation was established via partnerships with Toyota and Joe Gibbs Racing—the team Hamlin has driven for since 2005. Yes, Hamlin races against his own drivers on Sundays.

Wallace, who left Richard Petty's team and the famed No. 43 ride for 23XI, brought talent, charisma, brashness, social awareness heightened by involvement in the Black Lives Matter movement—and sponsors! McDonald's, Columbia Sportswear, DoorDash, Root Insurance, and Dr Pepper were founding sponsors; all except Dr Pepper followed him to 23XI. Wallace, astutely, called it, "an opportunity of a lifetime."

(ABOVE) **NBA Hall of Famer Michael Jordan, co-owner of 23XI Racing, watches from Watkins Glen's pit road during a 2021 race.**

(OPPOSITE) **Bubba Wallace (left) and Tyler Reddick (right) posed with former 23XI driver Kurt Busch at Darlington Raceway in 2023.**

"This is a new team," Hamlin cautioned at the start of 2021. "This is not an inherited team. This is a team built from scratch."

True, but considering the sponsors, Jordan, and Wallace, that sounded like a bit of good old-fashioned sandbagging.

Wallace got 23XI's first victory in October 2021 at Talladega Superspeedway. He was the second Black driver to win a Cup Series race. Wendell Scott was the first, back in 1963. Wendell never even got a trophy. Wallace got famous. Times are different, which is a good thing in this case.

Former Cup Series champion Kurt Busch came aboard in 2022 and, with a win at Kansas, qualified the team's second car into the NASCAR Playoffs before a crash at Pocono resulted in concussion-like symptoms, forcing Busch to miss the playoffs. He never returned, retiring in August 2023. Tyler Reddick took over the ride after 23XI bought out his contract with Richard Childress Racing, something Hamlin considered a coup. Reddick, a two-time Xfinity Series champion, and Wallace both made the playoffs in '23. And you have to like that the 2023 season started with a true maverick move, giving former Supercross/X Games star Travis Pastrana a one-off seat for the Daytona 500 a decade after his failed attempt at a NASCAR career. He started last. He finished eleventh.

Yes, this is serious.

"I thought [23XI coming in] was a really, really cool thing for the sport," said journalist Kelly Crandall, co-author of *NASCAR 75 Years*. "They're doing something different. The race name is really unique. They've used different paint schemes. And they're really trying to push diversity efforts."

And succeeding, with initiatives like the Dr Pepper 23XI SPEED Institute Tuition Program. The sponsor provides $5,000 in tuition to twenty-three deserving students from diverse backgrounds, with two students awarded internships by the Institute, which is 23XI Racing's "educational and professional development initiative." The NASCAR Drive for Diversity Awards honored 23XI three straight years, 2022 through '24, for its diversity and inclusion efforts.

Nice effort in 2023, putting former 24 Hours of Le Mans champion Kamui Kobayashi in a third car at the Indianapolis Motor Speedway road course race. Kobayashi finished thirty-third, as only the second Japanese driver to appear in the Cup Series. He called it "his dream," adding that he thinks his one-off can lead to more Japanese drivers coming to NASCAR.

At Talladega's spring 2024 race, the 23XI team got its sixth Cup victory, this one with Reddick driving. This time, Jordan was at-track. He joined in the Victory Lane celebration, lugging Riddick's young son Beau from trackside to see his father, all the while pumping his fists to the crowd.

"Well, Denny keeps saying I'm bad luck," Jordan said, "And today we proved him wrong. Everybody always tells me when we win, we have a good celebration, but this is the first time I've been here [for a win]. To me, this is like an NBA playoff game."

23XI, no doubt, is more than a name.

Martinsville Speedway, November 2022: Ross Chastain needed a last-lap miracle to finish high enough to qualify for the season-finale, NASCAR Cup Series championship race where four drivers would battle for the title. He came up with what is now called the "Hail Melon"--a nod to his family's watermelon farming business--by jamming his Chevrolet into the wall and simultaneously mashing the gas. That combo enabled the Chevy to turn a lap faster than the track's pole qualifying record! Chastain made up five spots to make the final four. Now that's a maverick!

ROSS CHASTAIN—"THE NEXT DALE EARNHARDT?"

ROSS CHASTAIN'S "ARRIVAL" in NASCAR's premier series actually came years after he started competing—courtesy of a bold and thrilling last-lap race move unlike anything ever seen in the highest level of NASCAR competition. In many ways, that extraordinary, desperate "Martinsville Move" sums up the gumption and drive of NASCAR's newest brand of stock car hero, one NASCAR Chairman and CEO Jim France calls "our next Dale Earnhardt."

From a family of eighth-generation Florida watermelon farmers, Chastain wasn't necessarily predisposed to a career in auto racing. But his presence there since getting a career-making chance in the big leagues has made him one of the most-talked about drivers.

Love him or hate him—and there are plenty of fans on either side—Chastain's "no prisoners" style of competition has absolutely elicited sentimental notions of a certain seven-time champion who similarly was fundamentally more focused on doing whatever it took to win races, not to win friends.

Chastain smiles about the comparisons with the late NASCAR Hall of Famer Dale Earnhardt, but concedes his uncommon grit hails from a different origin and time.

"I do hear some of the comparisons," Chastain allowed. "I never was fortunate enough to meet Dale Earnhardt. But when I drive, I'm just me.

"I try not to crash, try not to hit the wall, try not to run into people. I try to just beat them all. I definitely make my fair share of mistakes. But, yes, I've seen the transition from a lot of boos to a good amount of cheers. I'm not going to make everybody happy, but I'm just there to race and people see that."

They see that and have come to appreciate that.

In his first full-time NASCAR Cup Series season driving a championship-caliber car, Chastain essentially made modern history and even created his own lexicon executing a move on track dubbed the "Hail Melon"—a nod to his family's business.

To make the 2022 championship Final Four, Chastain needed to gain spots on the final lap of the penultimate playoff race at Martinsville Speedway. So, in a maneuver on track as audacious as it was desperate—Chastain turned his No. 1 Trackhouse Racing Chevrolet toward the retaining wall and floored the gas pedal for the final ½-mile lap.

Pressing his car against the wall and pressing the pedal to the floor, Chastain ran a lap quicker than the pole qualifying record to move up five positions on track and boldly take the final playoff position. It was among the most talked-about moves in NASCAR history, often referred to as a "video game move" because of its almost unbelievable reality.

Chastain's competitors climbed out of their cars that day shaking their heads in disbelief and asking, "What was that?" NASCAR Hall of Famer and race commentator Dale Earnhardt Jr. insisted on live television, "I've never seen anything like that." Even Formula 1 racers marveled on social media about Chastain's bold move.

The resulting position to compete for a championship ended in a runner-up finish the next week, and the "Hail Melon" was officially outlawed by NASCAR in the ensuing offseason. But Chastain's uncommon willingness to put it on the line made him a champion among many. And it established him as a driver to watch—a banner he'd never necessarily carried before.

"You make that move at Martinsville, amen, you're a maverick," said ESPN personality Ryan McGee. "That's just you; your brain isn't wired the same as us mere mortals. It's the reason they print T-shirts with their faces on them and they don't do T-shirts with my face on them. Because [Chastain], that's a maverick, right? That's just someone who's built different than the rest of us."

After spending his first four seasons at the NASCAR Cup Series level in underfunded, noncompetitive cars and another at Chip Ganassi Racing as the team was sold, Chastain—at last—earned a shot with a stable, title-bound team. And he's answered with an exceptional drive to prove what talent and commitment can produce. He won a pair of races in his first two seasons with Trackhouse Racing, qualifying for the playoffs both years.

If his unwavering single focus bothers his competitors, then Chastain believes they are off their game. He understands his bold style may agitate some, but he's also noticing it's appreciated by others.

"It's a race," Chastain reminded. "I don't want anybody to be mad at me on the track, but I also don't care if the guys I'm racing don't like me, because I'm there to beat them. If we all liked each other, we'd let each other win and then nobody would win.

"I just want to win, so if they get upset with that as racers, then great, that's cool.

"The things I'm trying to clean up are the moments I make a mistake and cause a crash. I don't want to cause crashes; I just want to beat them.

"It's a race at the end of the day."

One week after pulling off his controversial wall move at Martinsville, Chastain was waving to fans at Phoenix Raceway during the "Championship 4" driver introductions.

NASCAR RETURNS TO LE MANS

THE IMPACT OF the NASCAR Garage 56 entry in the 2023 one-hundredth running of the 24 Hours of Le Mans was easily evident even to the naked eye. The blue-and-black high-profile Chevrolet Camaro was, by far, the largest car in the field—literally standing out and above all the others even while sitting still on the starting grid—surreal scene among the other more traditional sports car entries.

And it wasn't just the amazing A-list of Garage 56 drivers—seven-time NASCAR Cup Series Champion Jimmie Johnson, Formula 1 champion Jenson Button, sports car champion Mike Rockenfeller, and reserve driver, popular IMSA champion Jordan Taylor—who were passionately cheered on all week in the center of sports car summer mecca, but the very car itself.

It stood out—the ultimate maverick.

Le Mans Lineup (from left): Four-time NASCAR Cup Series champion and current Hendrick Motorsports Vice Chairman Jeff Gordon, actor and former IMSA sports car racer Patrick Dempsey, IMSA President John Doonan, NASCAR Chairman/CEO Jim France and Hendrick Motorsports Vice President of Competition Chad Knaus gather at the 2023 race.

Its unmistakable presence was absolutely indicative of the phenomenal welcome back NASCAR received to the great international endurance race in June 2023—the first NASCAR entry there in fifty years.

The No. 24 Chevrolet Camaro ZL1—prepared and fielded by a dream team conglomeration of NASCAR, IMSA, Hendrick Motorsports, General Motors, and Goodyear—was the consistent talking point of the esteemed one hundred–year-old race through the bucolic French countryside.

From its first appearance at the race's Scrutineering event early week, where the entries undergo technical checks in the city's Place de la République in a festival-type atmosphere, fans couldn't get enough of the Garage 56 entry. Crowds ten and fifteen people deep surrounded the car and team absolutely everywhere they went in Le Mans.

Ultimately, extra track marshals were called in to help monitor all the well-wishers at the track. Fans were perpetually crowded behind the Garage 56 pit box and garage eagerly hoping to see the car and/or one of its celebrated drivers. The line for autographs the Thursday before the race was easily triple that of any other team on the grid, for so many the once-in-a-lifetime chance to meet a NASCAR champion like Johnson.

The following day's parade through the small tightly packed downtown Le Mans streets was as crowded as any local or longtime Le Mans fan could remember; the response and love for the Garage 56 team was remarkable.

Importantly, Garage 56 did not disappoint on track, maneuvering the famed 8.4-mile Circuit de le Sarthe. The car, in its own "experimental" class, was so fast it outqualified the entire GTE Am class by more than two seconds. The distinctive sound of the car was loud and rapturous—you heard it coming and you heard it going—eyesight not required.

Even with a slight hiccup overnight in the race—the Garage 56 team made repairs for drive line issues—it finished thirty-ninth in the sixty-two-car field completing 285 laps, each one distinct and memorable. It was a triumph of engineering but, as importantly, an international showcase for NASCAR ingenuity, technical expertise, and star power.

As the final laps reeled off, Champagne was poured in Garage 56. Executives from NASCAR, IMSA, General Motorsports, Hendrick Motorsports, and Goodyear gathered at the back of the team's increasingly crowded garage area at the end of pit road. The mass of fans was there. The legendary driver lineup was smiling.

A shot representing 75 years of maverick operatin': The Hendrick Motorsports Chevrolet Camaro ZR1 NASCAR entry sits in the apparent middle of the field, prior to the 24 Hours of Le Mans in 2023. Bill France Sr., in case you didn't know, would've been ecstatic about this.

Iconic race, iconic bridge, memorable photo: The number twenty-four NASCAR Next Gen Chevrolet ZL1 driven by Jimmie Johnson, Jenson Button and Mike Rockenfeller races under the Dunlop bridge at the Circuit de la Sarthe in the 2023 24 Hours of Le Mans.

And when that incredible No. 24 Chevrolet driven by seven-time NASCAR Champion Jimmie Johnson roared by to take the Le Mans one-hundredth anniversary checkered flag, the celebration began in earnest. There was nothing but feel-great emotions.

"It's beyond expectations," IMSA President John Doonan grinningly told reporters. "[NASCAR Chairman] Jim [France] had his expectations that we put NASCAR further on a global stage and satisfy our partners that were critical for this to happen.

"I think most rewarding for me was seeing all the men and women in this program experience this place, this event, especially it being the one-hundredth anniversary. I walk out of this circuit this evening with a whole new group of friends in this industry. And that's hard to come by."

As fireworks went off and the toasts began, there was no question about what this experience meant to all—to the executives, the drivers and their families, the devoted team of engineers and crew that spent almost two years working on the project. To the fans who got to see how much NASCAR's drive around the French countryside meant to so many.

"Pretty damn good," a smiling Johnson repeated.

And it was.

AFTERWORD

ROSS CHASTAIN

Racing in NASCAR was my dream from an early age. Growing up in the field as an eighth-generation farmer taught me the importance of hard work and determination, and I have carried that with me throughout my NASCAR career. Over the years, there have been countless ups and downs, but my unwillingness to give up is a testament to why I am still here today.

I owe it to my fans and sponsors, to my car owners, and to NASCAR to never give up, to race as hard as I can. Every lap, every race. The platform that I have as a NASCAR driver is built around performance, so never giving an inch matters. I look back to the all-time greats and draw inspiration from their attitudes.

I do things my way. Off the track, I embrace the opportunity to grow the sport of NASCAR. Signing autographs, doing appearances and speeches, working in the ag community, promoting highway safety—these are all blessings that being a NASCAR driver affords me.

But on the track, I am there to win.

I take risks and put my competitors in spots that benefit me. And sometimes that doesn't work. But I continue to learn, evolve, and adapt to be the best driver I can be.

Only a few years into my career in the NASCAR Cup Series, I race for an amazing organization in Trackhouse Racing. The sky is the limit on where we can go from here.

PHOTO CREDITS

A = All; T – Top; B = Bottom; L = Left; R = Right

The Associated Press: 124; **Chris Graythen/Getty Images:** 168; **Chris Trotman/Getty Images:** 151; **Clive Rose/Getty Images:** 183; **David Taylor/Getty Images:** 128; **Donald Miralle/Getty Images:** 164; **The Enthusiast Network/Getty Images:** 84; **Ezra Shaw:** 146; **Gerardo Mora/Getty Images:** 161; **Jared C. Tilton/Getty Images:** 153R, 175R, 178; **Jerry Markland/Getty Images:** 174; **Logan Riely/Getty Images:** 179; **Marc Piasecki/Getty Images:** 182; **NASCAR:** 8, 9, 10, 14, 15A, 16A, 17, 18, 19, 20, 21, 22, 23, 24, 25A, 26, 27A, 28, 29, 30A, 31, 33A, 34, 35, 36, 39, 41, 42, 43A, 44, 45, 46, 47A, 48, 49A, 50, 51, 53, 54, 55, 57, 58, 59, 60A, 61, 62, 63, 67, 69, 70, 71, 73, 74, 75, 76, 77, 78, 80, 81, 82, 83A, 87, 88A, 89A, 92, 93, 94, 95, 96, 99A, 100, 101, 105, 106A, 107, 108, 109, 113A, 115A, 116, 117, 118, 119, 120, 121, 122, 123A, 125, 126, 127, 131, 132A, 135A, 137L, 138, 139, 140T, 141, 142, 143, 149, 153L, 155A, 156, 157, 159, 163A, 165A, 166, 168, 171, 172, 173, 177L, 181; **Nigel Kinrade Photography:** 145; **Racing One/Getty Images:** 13, 40, 52, 64, 68, 97, 102, 111,112, 140B; **Robert Laberge/Getty Images:** 7; **Sarah Crabill/Getty Images:** 176; **Sean Gardner/Getty Images:** 167, 175L; **Stacey Revere/Getty Images:** 180; **Zuma Press, Inc./Alamy Stock Photo:** 177R.

INDEX

D

E

F

G

H

I

J

K

L

M

N

O

P

U

V

W

X

Y

Z